Stop Blaming the Fish

How <u>YOU</u> Affect Your Negotiated Outcomes

James J. Ranieri

Published by BookLocker.com, Inc., St. Petersburg, Florida.

Printed on acid-free paper.

Booklocker.com, Inc.
2017

First Edition

Dedicated to Dr. Kathryn Ranieri, my love, my partner, my inspiration, my moral compass and my center

Acknowledgements

I would like to thank my readers and friends, editor, family and everyone who played a part in this work. Specifically, I wish to acknowledge the contributions of my wife and partner in life, Dr. Kate Ranieri, for her encouragement, guidance, patience and belief in me. Thanks to our daughters, Emily and Francesca, and their families for participating in my grand experiment to teaching them how to negotiate as children. Special recognition again to Dr. Roland Dumas, for both contributing and serving as my compass to help me understand what I was trying to convey. My appreciation goes to Scott Bastian, Michael Ripple and Richard O'Hara for their feedback and contributing to the readability of this work. I extend a special thanks to my editor Sara Vigneri.

Table of Contents

A Fishing Story

The following is an adaptation of a parable from the Babylonian Talmud.

Once upon a time there was a selfish fisherman who fished in a beautiful lake stocked with an abundance of delicious fish. He had two mates to assist him on his boat with menial tasks, one who was lame and the other who was blind. He selected these two helpers because they were not capable of catching fish due to their disabilities. The fisherman was selfish and wanted to keep all of the fish for himself and he felt confident that their disabilities would prevent them from poaching his fish.

The owner of the boat went away for an extended time, but he did not make provisions for sustenance for the two mates. Near starvation the lame mate said to the blind mate: "I see many beautiful fish in the lake. Come, I will ride on your shoulders, and we will catch them and eat them together."

So the lame mate rode on the shoulders of the blind mate, and they caught and ate all of the fish in the lake.

Days later the fisherman returned and noticed that there were no more fish in the lake. He was furious and asked, "Where are all my splendid fish?" The lame mate replied, "Because you left us with no food we were starving. Have I feet to walk with?" The blind mate replied, "Have I eyes to see with? Acting as one, we were able to catch and eat the fish to keep us from starving." The fisherman became extremely angry, and blamed the mates. He failed to recognize that by not providing food for the mates he had driven them to take matters into their own hands and behave in a way that he had not anticipated.

Like the fisherman, you may attempt to conjure lame excuses, blinded by your self-interests by blaming others or making excuses for problems created by your own doing.

Foreword

"The best way to predict the future is to create it."

Peter Drucker

Our attention span seems to have collapsed, such that a single transaction encompasses an eternity. While writing this book, I have been concerned that it may seem too counterintuitive or even out of step with today's new reality because of a pervasive 'ends justifying the means' mentality. The path ahead can seem daunting given the recent seismic shifts toward national interests trumping massive global problems, the increasing polarity among political ideologies and religious traditions and the erosion of civility. To be truthful, I wonder if what I am espousing in this book is passé, but I believe that the pendulum has again reached an extreme limit and it will eventually equilibrate back to the center. Tomorrow the sun will again rise in the East, set in the West and cooler heads will prevail. The need for the lessons of this book will continue to increase as people recognize the illusion of permanence and accept that change is in fact the only constant in life.

Chapter I - Stop Blaming The Fish

"He who knows others is wise. He who knows himself is enlightened."

Lao Tzu

As in the fisherman fable, life offers countless examples of how we tend to justify our own actions and blame others for our problems. We point fingers of blame to everyone except ourselves. Have you ever fished and come away with a less than expected catch and said the fish aren't biting? Why blame the fish? It couldn't be your fault that you didn't catch enough fish. Could it?

Blaming someone or something for our own failures is called scapegoating. Scapegoating uses projection and displacement to focus feelings of aggression, hostility and frustration on someone else. The amount of blame assigned is usually disproportionate and unwarranted. Thoughts and feelings are usually unconsciously projected on another person and they become the scapegoat for problems of our own doing. Whether we get into the wrong lane of traffic, or end up on the slowest check-out line, most of us have developed a core competence in scapegoating by finding someone or something else to blame for problems we create.

The disgruntled fisherman with no catch needs to ask some fundamental questions. Who chose to go fishing on that particular day, in that exact spot, using that bait and equipment? It wasn't the fish. It was the fisherman. By analogy, you may look at negotiations in much the same way. If a deal falls through you might find yourself making excuses, such as, the other person was a better negotiator, or was deceptive, or tricked me or did something unethical. Or, you might claim that the deal didn't come together because someone stacked the deck against you or that the circumstances surrounding the negotiation were not in your favor.

Some people make these excuses because they are either not comfortable with or do not understand how to negotiate. On the flip side, bully negotiators face a completely different set of problems as a consequence of their negotiating style. They may question, why don't people trust me? Why doesn't anyone help me when I need help? Why is he waiting so long to get back at me? When they find themselves on the short end of the stick they rationalize by saying, "sometimes you get the dog and sometimes the dog gets you." In either case, you rarely, if ever, examine why negotiations turn out the way they do.

So let's start with YOU. Why aren't you the best negotiator you can be? Do you tend to give in too easily or push too hard? Is maintaining a good relationship more important than getting a better deal, or the converse? Do you avoid negotiating situations or seek them out? Do people tend to take advantage of you or avoid dealing with you? Does your empathy for others or lack of it get in the way of getting what you need? Do you approach living from a perspective of scarcity or plenty?

The core messages in this book are "know thyself" and "you are responsible for what happens to you." A negotiation usually gives you three moving parts to deal with; yourself, the counterpart and the situation. Knowing yourself and taking responsibility is important and it's worth diagnosing your overlearned responses. Understanding yourself gives rise to understanding your counterpart. Negotiating situations are driven by environment in the search to find common ground. *Stop Blaming the Fish* is a focused look at how YOU affect our negotiated outcomes, not others, not tricks and ploys, not theories, not tactics or mind games.

Here's what lies ahead. This book will both start and end with you. You will examine your overlearned responses and your comfort zone. Next, you will take a deep dive into what drives perceptions and understand different styles that you will encounter when you negotiate with a counterpart. You will become aware of your default personality traits (and the default traits of others) and assess if they are assets or liabilities. You will evaluate yourself along the continuums of five separate personality styles. Finally, based on your personal needs, you'll develop a tailored game plan of what YOU can specifically do to improve your negotiated results. I hope you find *Stop Blaming the Fish* enlightening. If you're usually not happy with your negotiated results, it's time to take control and Stop Blaming the Fish.

Chapter II - What's On Your Hook?

"We don't see things as they are, we see them as we are."

Anais Nin

Most fishermen have a favorite lure or bait that they use to catch fish. Good fishermen understand that even though they have an attachment to that one lure or bait, it cannot be used to catch all types of fish in all cases. They need to adjust to the situation. By analogy, based upon how we see the world, we tend to favor certain types of behavior, like that lure or bait that we trust and are most comfortable with. The problem is that how we behave in a particular situation is generally reactive and rarely challenged. Like the lure, our worldview has value. But it drives our actions unconsciously, which has limits and serious liabilities.

In his book *Doing Documentary Work*, Robert Coles, physician, philosopher and documentarian, used the term location to describe a conceptual lens a documentarian takes on a particular project. The "What" you document is objective, the "How" is subjective. Your subjective filters define your location. The purpose of understanding location is threefold; first to make sense of what you discern, then how to decide on what to process and finally how to process the information. Understanding your location, whether in creating a documentary or negotiating a resolution requires you to take stock of who you are. Location is rarely static. It varies with your knowledge and emotional state of being.

In negotiations, location serves as your unique lens through which to see, or your personal world-view. Location constitutes the totality of your perceptions. It filters and creates mentally imprinted evaluation models. Your location defines your framework for seeing, evaluating, assigning meaning and acting on situations you encounter. It is your viewing point and is the total of everything that you believe, value and choose to be etched in your brain.

The intersection of multiple factors defines your individual location. Those factors may include your personal values, rituals, fears, personality elements, traditions, gender identity, spirituality, ethnicity, beliefs, experiences, morality, intelligence and generational cohort.

They form the multifaceted lens by which you evaluate and assign meaning to any situation. The processes that your brain employs are both explicit and implicit, or conscious and unconscious, although the majority of processes are unconscious.

Much of your location comes without your consent. That is, you rarely choose the components of your location. DNA, families, friends and the communities in which you live contribute a significant portion of what is programmed and imprinted into your brain. It is imperative that you take stock of yourself to consciously understand your location and avoid unwittingly drifting through life and negotiations.

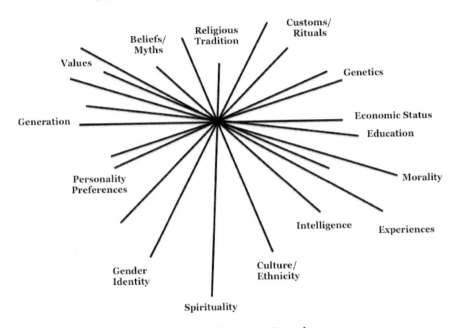

Contributing Factors to Location

This diagram is a visualization of what contributes to your location. Your location resides at the intersection of all of these components. The intent is to get better insight into those elements that drive perceptions. The elements that constitute your location are not equal in magnitude and vary widely from person to person. You determine what is meaningful by your location. You tend to notice things based on your location. Location will evolve and change based on your development, state of mind, or moods. An analysis of each element of your location would constitute a life's work. So, I will limit the further discussion of location to a single component, your personality traits, because of the absolutely critical impact they have on how you negotiate.

Please understand that personality traits are a dynamic set of characteristics that uniquely influence cognition, emotion, motivation, and behavior. Over time, your personality traits consistently affect your patterns of thoughts, feelings, social adjustments, and behaviors unless conscious efforts to change are made. It strongly drives your perceptions, expectations, reactions and attitudes. If understood, they can also accurately predict your response to situations.

To help you understand how your personality traits affect how you negotiate, I'll introduce you to a personality assessment tool, the Global Five. Coupled with this book, it will help you in assessing your needs for relationship, information, structure, information sharing as well as your emotional response as they relate to negotiating. Go to http://similarminds.com/ global5/g5-jung.html where you can access the Global Five Assessment for free.

Overview of the Global Five
Academic research points to only five purely independent personality elements. Every personality trait will have some correlation with one or more of these five key elements. But what you score on one independent element says nothing about what you will score on another independent element. The Global/Big Five personality system is based on the five proven independent elements that have been empirically found in multiple cultures. Most elements correlate with other traditional psychometric instruments such as the Myers-Briggs Type Indicator (MBTI) and DiSC. A major difference of the Global Five versus MBTI and DiSC is that the personality elements do not affect one another.

The Global Five is an adaption of the Big Five personality traits, also known as the five-factor model (FFM); a model based on common language descriptors of personality. These descriptors are grouped together using a statistical technique called factor analysis. The five factors are openness to experience, conscientiousness, extraversion, agreeableness, and neuroticism. Beneath each proposed factor are more specific factors. For example, extraversion is said to include such related qualities as gregariousness, assertiveness, excitement seeking, warmth, activity, and positive emotions.

The Big Five personality traits were modeled to explain the relationship between personality and behaviors. This model was defined by several independent sets of researchers. These researchers began by studying relationships between large numbers of known personality traits, reducing the lists of these traits and then determining the underlying factors of personality.

The Global Five measures Extroversion, Orderliness, Emotional Stability, Accommodation, and Intellect. These elements make up the fabric of personality; the combination of elements in each person yields their overall personality trait profile. There are 32 possible combinations of these elements and ten primary types. The scale is linear and represents the relative strength of the trait. For example, if you scored 84 in Accommodation that means you have a high propensity to be very accommodating. But if you scored 20 it means that you have strong Egocentric traits.

Each of the five elements has two polar opposite extremes, as shown. A sample of the Global Five is displayed as you see below (they happen to be my results). I have found the instrument to generate highly repeatable results that are relatively constant over the last few years, unlike several other psychometrics.

Global Five Test Results

Extroversion	|||||||||||||||||||||||	78%
Orderliness	|||||||||||||||||||||||||	80%
Emotional Stability	|||||||	36%
Accommodation	||||||||||||||||	60%
Inquisitiveness	|||||||||||||||||||	68%

<u>S</u>ocial versus <u>R</u>eserved

Social types exhibit extroversion that projects energy, positive emotions, impulsiveness, assertiveness, sociability, the tendency to seek stimulation in the company of others, and talkativeness. High extraversion is often perceived as attention seeking, and domineering. Low extraversion causes a reserved, reflective personality, which can be seen as aloof or self-absorbed. The Global Five Test Results of Extroversion at 78% indicates highly Social tendencies.

- Social types feel at ease and are energized by interacting with others
- Reserved types may feel uncomfortable, disinterested and at times overwhelmed with social interaction

Impact of Being Social or Reserved

It's no surprise that Social people are extraverted and Reserved people tend to be more Introverted. Let's take a moment to define a few terms before you move on. The words Introverts and Extraverts do not simply mean brash and bold or shy and retiring. At the core of these two descriptors is how a person is energized.

People energize Social types. They tend to talk to think. Their energy is built by engaging, being with and interacting with other people. It has a catalytic effect on social people. Sociability is both a negotiating asset and liability. It's an asset in that Socials can project confidence, charisma, and likability. The liability for extreme, over-energized Socials, is that they tend to talk too much. This can result in saying the wrong thing during a negotiation, sharing too much information and dominating conversations. This leads to giving away intelligence instead of gaining insights.

Unlike social people, reserved people tend to think to talk. Someone who is reserved tends to need to go inside and recharge him or herself when a complex issue confronts them. Their social analogs need to recharge by going outside themselves. Again, like being social, being reserved is both an asset and liability in a negotiation. Reserved behavior prevents you from inadvertently divulging sensitive information. In the extreme, reserved people can appear to be cold, anti-social and aloof.

<u>O</u>rganized versus <u>U</u>nstructured

A tendency to be organized and dependable, show self-discipline, act dutifully, aim for achievement and prefer planned rather than spontaneous behavior. High conscientiousness is often perceived as stubborn and obsessive. Low conscientiousness can be flexible and spontaneous but can be perceived as sloppy and unreliable. The Global Five Test Results of Orderliness at 80% indicates highly organized.

- Organized types are focused
- Unstructured types appear scattered

Impact of Being Organized versus Unstructured

Organized people prefer to have everything in its proper place, things to work as planned and completed on schedule. Unstructured people tend to enjoy perfecting, exploring, and spontaneity. They like being unpredictable; it's sport to them. Ambiguity does not bother them. Again, taken to extremes both of these behavioral preferences can have consequences in negotiating. Some can be devastating.

In negotiating, the most organized person tends to be well prepared. Deadlines and commitments drive them, and that results in having a heightened need for closure. Under pressure, they may make large concessions to close the deal. Conversely, they may walk away from a negotiation if they mistakenly interpret the actions of an unstructured person as not working in good faith. An overly organized person can appear to be too tightly buttoned. This trait projects them as being onerous, overbearing, inflexible and not collaborative.

In contrast, the unstructured person tends to wing it; they fly by the seat of their pants relying on their wits and instinct. They enjoy using the element of surprise in negotiations, which can be interpreted as unpredictable and can severely erode trust. Since they tend not to waste time in preparing, they can be extremely frustrating in a negotiation because their actions seem random. Their need to continuously refine and perfect an agreement can cause them to blow deals that are achievable. Their personal preferences and behaviors compounded by a lack of preparation can make them appear to be disjointed, scattered, unfocused and insincere.

Limbic versus Calm

The Limbic tend to experience unpleasant emotions easily, such as anger, anxiety, depression, and vulnerability. They are more transparent and therefore easily readable. Emotional Stability also refers to impulse control. A high need for stability manifests as a stable and calm personality, but can be seen as uninspiring and unconcerned. Those with a low need for stability are reactive, excitable and often very dynamic individuals, but they can be perceived as unstable or insecure. The Global Five Test Results of Emotional Stability at 36% indicates Limbic, reactive tendencies.

- Limbic types are prone to variable, moody and reactive behavior
- Calm types maintain level emotions

Impact of Being Calm versus Limbic

Fact or myth: Are a person's eyes the window to their soul? Many people believe that this is true. How many times in your life have you heard someone significant say, "look me in the eye and tell me ...," as if they could read your mind by looking into your eyes. The fact is that a person's pupils do dilate based upon the type of visual information presented. A picture of a scantily dressed woman will generally cause the pupil of a man to dilate, while a picture of an attractive male will cause most women's pupils to do the same. When shown a picture of something disagreeable or threatening both men and women tend to squint to try and shut out the image. However, it is a myth that you can read someone's intent by looking into his or her eyes. Pupil dilation is indicative of comfort or discomfort, not truth or deception. Some people may be uncomfortable with staring into someone's eyes, but it doesn't necessarily mean that they are being deceptive.

The eyes, like the rest of the body, are governed by the limbic system. But before you consider if being calm or limbic affects your negotiations, some baseline level setting needs to occur. This will keep us from making false assessments. Regardless of demonstrating limbic or calm behavior preferences both prefrontal cortex and limbic functions are essential to survival. Relying on one over others can have some significant consequences in negotiating. So, let's take a look at what they do and then how it potentially impacts your negotiated outcomes.

The structures of the limbic system form the primitive brain. They are implicated in motivation, emotion, learning, and memory. The limbic system operates by influencing the endocrine and the autonomic nervous systems. The endocrine system is an information signal system like the nervous system. The nervous system sends information very quickly, and responses are short lived. The autonomic nervous system is a control system that acts unconsciously. It regulates bodily functions such as the heart rate, digestion, respiratory rate, pupil response and sexual arousal. The limbic system primarily controls the fight-or-flight response and the freeze-and-dissociate response. It is largely a reactive, involuntary system that requires no conscious thought. These reactions are a hard-wired program that automatically trigger a reaction intended to protect us from threats.

The prefrontal cortex region has been implicated in planning complex cognitive behaviors, personality expression, decision-making, and moderating social behavior. The basic activity of this brain region is considered to be the orchestration of thoughts and actions by internal goals.

The frontal cortex area is the evolved human brain. It executes its executive function such as the ability to differentiate among conflicting thoughts, determine good and bad, better and best, same and different, future consequences of current activities, working toward a defined goal, prediction of outcomes, expectation based on actions, and social "control." It supports concrete rule learning. More anterior regions of frontal cortex support rule learning at higher level of abstraction. The frontal cortex gives people the abilities to perceive emotions, use emotions, understand emotions and manage emotions. It is the reasoning part of the brain and allows us to remain calm.

Early humans, both male and female, relied almost exclusively on the limbic system. As humans evolved, the prefrontal cortex evolved, but did not replace the limbic system. Both are essential to conducting and navigate our daily lives. Neither is subordinate or superior when it comes to our survival. They both perform markedly different and vital functions.

At its root, a limbic behavior is reactive, reflexive and automatic. Polygraphs rely on the limbic bodily responses to determine deviation from a baseline. Polygraph machines are used in police work to ascertain if someone is telling the truth or attempting to deceive. If you're like most people, lying makes your heart rate accelerate, alters your breathing patterns, drives up your blood pressure and makes you sweat. A polygraph machine detects lies by looking for signs of these physiological changes. The first step in the polygraph process is to establish a baseline. A series of non-threatening questions are asked, and the subject's sensual responses are recorded through a series of sensors wired to the subject. Then, the subject is asked questions related to the investigation.

If the subject's responses vary significantly from the baseline, a skilled polygraph operator will redirect and drill questions to unearth the subject's level of discomfort. Polygraphs are not absolute in determining truth or deception, but gauge comfort or discomfort. However, without establishing a baseline, the polygraph operator would not be able to interpret the results of the test.

Like a polygraph machine, you can detect comfort or discomfort during a negotiation by observing a person's body language. According to psychologist Paul Ekman, no single behavior is indicative of deception. Behaviors that are often mistaken for dishonesty are primarily manifestations of stress. Even those who are truly gifted at detecting deception (which is only 1 percent of the population) are seldom right more than 60 percent of the time. Most of us are amateurs that rely on hunches and myths. What follows is not intended to be a short course on detecting discomfort in others, but rather to create awareness of how your unconscious limbic responses may be sending signals of discomfort and be misinterpreted by a novice hack as deception.

Joe Navarro, an ex-FBI agent, has written a compelling book, *What Every Body is Saying,* on non-verbal communications. If you are serious about understanding non-verbal cues I suggest you read it. Navarro debunks many myths that have become conventional wisdom in the art of people watching. Later I'll discuss how to protect yourself from body language pitfalls in negotiations but here are a few of the major take-a-ways. Like the polygraph, you need a baseline of behavior and response to determine relative comfort or discomfort using body language. Body language transmits discomfort of stress, not deception. Your limbic system is the initiator of nonverbal activity. You're largely blind to the non-verbal cues that you send. The hierarchical control of your non-verbal cues goes from the bottom to the top of your body. You have the least control over your feet, followed by your torso, then your hands, neck and finally your head. So the feet, not the eyes, are the greatest indicator of discomfort. Deviation from baseline behavior signals either a high level of comfort or discomfort. Most of us use a variety of quirky, unconscious, pacifying or soothing behaviors in times of comfort/discomfort. They may include whistling, constant rubbing, excessive yawning, blinking and twitching. Based upon the baseline, they are expressing a comfort/discomfort signal. Profuse sweating, extremely rapid speech, and hard swallowing are also telltales to explore. Again, do not assume that if someone doesn't look you in the eye, they are trying to deceive. Some personality types and ethnic cultures don't appreciate the direct use of eye contact or find eye contact distracting.

Pay attention to what your body is doing without your conscious involvement. It could be unwittingly giving clues about your reactions. Let me share an example. Years ago, I was involved in a negotiation for an extremely critical raw material of very high value to my company. What made the situation interesting from a negotiating standpoint was that the material was of relatively low value to the supplier. The long-term supply contract was expiring so it needed to be renegotiated. The existing agreement was a great deal that provided our company with very low cost material, but there had been a change of ownership at the supplier, so I entered the negotiations with lots of apprehensions.

We had defined our needs and wants and had anticipated what the supplier might need and request. As in most long-term contracts, published indices were used as escalators to determine future costs. We wanted to avoid using an energy-based index because the energy market was very turbulent at that time. As we entered into face-to-face negotiations with the supplier we exchanged niceties, presented our agenda and began substantive discussions. Each time the word energy was mentioned during the negotiation, my partner Ned started to tap his fingers on the table indicating that he was uncomfortable with discussing energy. Luckily, our counterparts did not pick up on that less than subtle clue and we eventually settled our negotiation without an index reflective of energy costs. But had they picked up on Ned's non-verbal response, the supplier's team stood the chance of receiving a windfall from the material that they sold to our company.

The term poker face refers to someone that shows no emotion. It's called poker face because while playing the game of poker it would be foolish to show any emotional behavior that might tip your hand and blow the game for you. Image a person frowning if they were dealt a lousy hand of cards or someone beaming if dealt a straight flush. Keeping a poker face prevents you from tipping your hand and allows you to bluff. But a poker face strategy should be extended to the entire body, not just the face. The term directs us to the wrong place to look. If you are prone to "happy feet" or other unconscious gestures involving the lower extremities then always sit behind a table.

A little-known fact about President Dwight D. Eisenhower is that he was an excellent poker player. During his military years, he had honed his skill and had built a notorious reputation for being able to bluff flawlessly. In *Ike's Bluff*, author Evan Thomas presents a chilling account of how the underrated Eisenhower, using the bluffing skill he had acquired in the Army, saved the world from a nuclear holocaust several times.

According to Thomas, upon assuming the presidency in 1953, Eisenhower worked to honor his campaign promise to end the Korean War. Many viewed him as a political lightweight. What they didn't see was that behind the bland smile and simple speech was a master strategists and tactician. Eisenhower took massive risk by bluffing that he might use nuclear weapons against the People's Republic of China (PRC) to end the Korean hostilities. Concurrently, he curbed his generals and advisors who favored the nuclear strikes. In the balance, Ike's gamble had only two possible consequences: thousands of lives saved, or millions of lives lost. He used the same strategy to keep the Soviets out of Western Europe. He threatened the Soviets that any move against Western Europe would be met with all the force at his disposal. He used this same approach to defuse the call for a preemptive nuclear strike on the Union of Soviet Socialist Republic (USSR) by the US with the same results. To this day, no one knows if Ike was bluffing about the use of nuclear weapons against the PRC or the USSR. A bluff is only viable if you are the only one that knows that you are bluffing.

Being calm and maintaining a cool, stoic posture may protect you from telegraphing your emotions or discomfort, but may come up short on relationship building. There's another downside to the poker face; being stoic makes you seem constant or frozen. Humans usually respond to particular stimuli with an appropriate response. If that response is suppressed, it looks weird. Constancy is abnormal behavior and is stressful to experience thereby creating doubt, distrust and confusion in the minds of those observing it. It throws people off to the point that they feel uncomfortable. The perception of being cold, cool, calm and calculating at the card table may be okay, but if you are trying to build trust and rapport with others at the negotiating table exclusively maintaining your game face might prove to be suboptimal.

Accommodating versus Egocentric
Accommodators have a tendency to be compassionate and cooperative rather than suspicious and antagonistic towards others. It is also a measure of one's trusting and helpful nature, and whether a person is generally well tempered or not. High agreeableness is often seen as naive or submissive. Low agreeableness can be seen as argumentative or untrustworthy because they are often competitive or challenging. The Global Five Test Results of Accommodation at 60% indicates moderate Accommodating tendencies.
- Accommodating types live for others
- Egocentric types live for themselves

Impact of Being Accommodating versus Egocentric
The Accommodating versus Egocentric personality trait is relatively self-explanatory, but has the greatest impact on your negotiations. The trait measures your propensity to trade Relationship (the need to nurture personal bonds) for Gain (the need for power) and vice versa. The stronger your Accommodating score, the more likely you will drive to keep the relationship in good shape at the expense of giving up potential gain. It follows that the lower the Accommodating score, the more likely it is that you will gravitate to Gain over Relationship. Whether conscious or unconscious, the only tradeoffs in negotiations are Relationship and Gain. This dynamic tension between these dipoles is always in play in negotiations. My purpose in discussing it is to ensure your trade-offs are being made consciously.

In my lectures and workshops I use a business school favorite called the Ultimatum Game to demonstrate how Relationship and Gain trade-off can be predicted by the strength or weakness of a person's Accommodating score. After administering the Global Five, I pair the person with the lowest Accommodation score (Player A) with the person scoring the highest in Accommodation (Player B). Remember the higher the Accommodation score, the more like a person is to default to Relationship at the expense of Gain. I present Player A with an envelope containing money. Player B does not know how much money is in the envelope. Usually, it's $25 to $50. The Players have two minutes to prepare and execute three rounds of offers to come to a resolution on how to divide the money. At the end of the third round the money is returned to me, and neither player gets anything if they cannot agree on how to divide what's in the envelope. Player A can only make offers and Player B can only accept or reject Player A's offers. If Player B accepts Player A's offer, they split the money as agreed. At the end of three rounds, if Player B rejects all of Player A's offers, then neither player gets any money. I caution both players not to worry about being fair, cooperative or exhibiting reciprocity. The sole object is to maximize what you get for both players.

That's the game, but here's what usually happens. The people with the lower Accommodation score will more than likely get more money (Gain) than people with higher Accommodation scores. People with higher Accommodation scores tend to settle on the first or second offer to demonstrate fairness and equitability (Relationship). Regardless of whom I give the money to the results turn out the same. If I give the envelope to the person with the higher Accommodation score, then their initial offer will be higher than people with low Accommodation scores. In summary, people with lower Accommodation scores get more money than those with higher scores. People with higher scores make higher initial offers and settle quickly.

So what does this all mean? Your Accommodation score is a reliable indicator of you natural propensity to trade Gain for Relationship or Relationship for Gain. Using the Global Five, as an indicator of that propensity is simple, the higher the Accommodation scores the greater the inclination to trade Gain for Relationship. My personality type is SLOAI. Here are the traits associated with that type.

Open, organized, asks lots of questions, outgoing, prone to panic, easily hurt, narcissistic, detail oriented, concerned about others, the first to act, believes that children need firm discipline, finishes most everything they start, comfortable around others, upset by misfortune of strangers, socially skilled, compliments others frequently, interested in people, busy, interested in the problems of others, tense, physically affectionate, overly nice, likes to lead, generous, in touch with feelings, not afraid to draw attention to self, manipulative, prone to jealousy, worrying, easily excited, motivated by the desire for acclaim, prone to addiction, frequently driven to impress others, passionate about causes, swayed by emotions, curious, anxious, passionate about bettering the world's condition, stressed, keeps spaces clean, believes in human goodness, well informed, thoughtful, assertive, fears doing the wrong thing, rushed

So what do these characteristics say about me as a negotiator? This list of attributes is common to all who share the SCOAI type. Not all the attributes are equal in magnitude. You must overlay the chart on page 11, which shows the relative strength of the trait, to make some sense out of this description. On that chart my score for Accommodation was 60%. That's a moderately high preference toward relationship. Over many years of negotiating, I have come to understand that my default is to trade Gain for Relationship to maintain harmony and well-being. I have also learned not to be a pushover and temper my responses in negotiation. I have been able to control my natural, hard-wired inclinations to acquiesce successfully, but it has not been easy. Here's the bottom line, the higher your Accommodation score, the more likely you feel a natural urge to default to Relationship at the sacrifice of Gain.

Non-curious versus Inquisitive
Inquisitives have an appreciation for art, emotion, adventure, unusual ideas, curiosity, and a variety of experience. Openness reflects someone's degree of intellectual curiosity, creativity and a preference for novelty and variety. It is also described the extent to which a person is imaginative or independent, and depicts a personal preference for a range of activities over a strict routine. Highly curious people can be

perceived as unpredictable or lacking focus. Moreover, individuals with high inquisitiveness are said to pursue self-actualization specifically by seeking out intense, euphoric experiences, such as skydiving, living abroad, gambling, et cetera. Conversely, those with low openness strive to gain fulfillment through perseverance and are characterized as pragmatic and data-driven—sometimes even perceived to be dogmatic and closed-minded. Some disagreement remains about how to interpret and contextualize the inquisitive factor. The Global Five Test Results of Inquisitiveness at 68% indicates moderately high Inquisitiveness.

- Non-curious types are more grounded in reality and less intellectually driven
- Inquisitive types are insatiable in their quest to know more

Impact of Being Inquisitive versus Non-curious

Non-curious people tend to be concrete, identify relevant facts and act based on logic. They determine realistic constraints, devise and implement incremental solutions. Non-curious people tend to question and are suspect of radical new approaches. They rely heavily on their five senses to take in information and gravitate toward information that is real and tangible. They observe the specifics of what is going on around them. When solving problems non-curious people tend to start with specifics and formulate a general case to explain it. They are especially attuned to realities, are practical and realistic, tend to focus on details and may ignore the big picture. They also tend to be literal in their words and would rather act than think.

Inquisitives tend to be dreamers and try to consider all possibilities. An Inquisitive likes to brainstorm alternatives, solve multiple problems at the same time, consider the future and identify trends and patterns. They trust their gut, hunches and instinct over data. When solving problems inquisitives try to make the specifics comply with a general case they have already identified. They focus on conceptual information and see the big picture but often tend to ignore the details. They strive to be attuned to seeing new possibilities, focus on the future and would rather think than do.

So what? When two people are at opposite ends of the detail/concept spectrum, it's as if they are speaking two markedly different languages. Their styles of problem solving are usually polar opposites. At its best, these differences can create confusion. At its worst, it can result in a complete communication breakdown and mutual distrust.

Your needs for relationship, information, structure, information sharing as well as your emotional response define you, your negotiating style and your default or fail safe hard wiring. Now, if you haven't done so, go online and take the 55 questions Global Five Assessment. Be sure to print your results for reference. The next section provides personal strategies for change. If you're usually not happy with your negotiated results, it's time to take control and Stop Blaming the Fish.

Chapter III - Charting Your Course

"Doubt is not a pleasant condition, but certainty is an absurd one."

Voltaire

Expert fishermen are not random in their skills or behaviors. They don't throw a line in the water haphazardly and expect to catch their limit. They have knowledge that provides the foundation to build their skill base. They are prepared and systematic. They understand and maintain their equipment. They select and use the right lure or bait for the type of fish they desire. They know where to drop their line. They understand how weather affects their chances to catch fish. Yet conditions arise that defy the preparation and knowledge of the best fisherman.

Understanding your personality traits and propensities to act in particular ways is a good start toward being a better negotiator. What follows will assist you in being able to predict reactions and outcomes to uncertain situations with better accuracy. How much better is dependent on the quality and quantity of information and the rigor that goes into your analysis. There are three models that you need to understand before you explore predicting how you and others affect negotiations. First, you need to be familiar with the negotiating cycle, a cause and effect model, of the various actions that lead to the success or failure of your negotiation. Second, you must have a grasp of the markedly different styles and where you tend to fit on the negotiating spectrum. Lastly, you examine the stupid stuff that people do as a substitute for logical thinking. Let's get started.

Negotiating Cycle

Negotiating is a resolution process that can temporarily settle issues between people and groups of people. Problems and issues are caused by perceived differences and change, not similarities. For a negotiation to be successful all the people involved must get what they need without irreparable damage to the relationship. A negotiation occurs when two or more parties have agreed to make a decision that affects each party differently, and the actual decision has not yet been made.

19

Purchases and contracts are obvious, but decisions on having children, where to spend vacations, or which concert to attend are all negotiating situations. You've decided that you will agree on something, have different notions of what a good solution is, and ready, set, go.

Some of us are accommodating and give in too quickly; others are egocentric and push too far. Few of us seem to get it right and navigate a situation by keeping Gain and Relationship in the right balance. Is this because of skill or experience? Partially, but I firmly believe that the reason this happens is more fundamental. It's our hardwiring. It's driven by the way you see and respond to the world. The truth is that you are largely unaware of the way you perceive a situation, form expectations and react. What follows is intended to help you understand why people see the same exact situation very differently, come to vastly different conclusions, and react in a multitude of ways resulting in a tremendous array of consequences.

All trade-offs in negotiations can be categorized as either perceived Relationship or perceived Gain. It would seem like an easy task to keep Relationship and Gain in balance, but in practice, it's an incredibly difficult task. The word perceived is key because it defines a person's reality. Two important dynamic forces affect the proper balance between Gain and Relationship. The first is our perception, and other is the context in which the situation exists. The difficulty of managing the equity between Relationship and Gain is that people have different perceptions of the value. For example, an invite to the Super Bowl is much more valuable to a football fan than someone who is not interested in sports. Gain is much easier to quantify than its qualitative counterpart of Relationship. Rarely, if ever, does a formula or equation determine equity between Gain and Relationship. Regrettably, both Gain and Relationship are always subject to human interpretation. Both are never garnered freely; they always come at price.

The second force is that perceived Gain and Relationship are contextually bound. In a negotiating situation the parties each have their spheres of interest. The negotiating space lies in the overlap of those two spheres. In that overlap of interest (picture a Venn diagram), is the domain of shared interest or common ground. The overlap can be large (married couple) or contain only the negotiation subject (car salesman). The larger the shared interest area, the more important

Relationship is in the negotiation. Solving for a "win" when Relationship is critical will ultimately cost a lot more than you bargained for. On the other hand, when the overlap is one item, the transaction in progress, solving for Relationship results in a loss. The car salesman will always share family stories and ask about your kids, right?

Since our lives are in a permanent state of flux, things are constantly changing. Some things are more stable and change at near glacial speed; others accelerate at the rate of the technologies that support them. A further complicating factor is that humans strive for permanence and stability and resist change. But we crave and cling to impermanent states and things, which is called 'dukkha' in the Buddhist tradition. So, when you strike an agreement you want it to be permanent, but permanence is not emblematic of our reality. You fight to maintain your Gains even though the situation, the context that enabled you to secure the agreement, is no longer in force. These factors are endemic to the human condition, and are inconsistent with life today.

So, where do you start? Let's look at what makes people different. The most distinctive attribute of man, beyond opposable thumbs, is our evolved brain. Here's a very brief primer on the aspects of the brain, an incredibly complex organ that affects all human interaction as it relates to negotiations. The human brain is similar to a 3-pound computer made of meat. Unlike a normal computer, it is not merely a simple input/output device. In addition to processing information with a preprogrammed algorithm, the brain's operating system manages the unconscious actions of our bodies, learns, communicates, evaluates, acts and stores mental models. Modern science reinforces that you come into the world with not only an operating system but some preprogrammed applications as well. Through the interaction of trillions of interconnected circuits and feedback loops, this amazing organ learns and stores new decision models. It is highly unlikely that two human brains are programmed in the same way. Each of us sees and processes things differently. This variability in seeing and processing explains, in part, the fundamental differences in perception.

Just like visible light is an extremely tiny component of the electromagnetic spectrum, we are only aware of a minuscule portion of what goes on in our brains minute by minute. According to David Eagleman, in his book *Incognito – The Secret Lives of the Brain*, most of our brain activity is unconscious. The information stored in our unconscious brain is dark data. You are not only unaware of it, but have no access to it. The unconscious working of the brain is analogous to a computer operating system. Its dark data is stealth and runs in the background autonomously. You don't see or interact with it. However, our conscious brain is like an application program. It executes specific functions and its operations are visible to us. Regrettably, much of the intentional mental actions you do in daily life are on autopilot and most of the time you are not even mindful of the fact that they are running. Take riding a bicycle. You are not aware of all the laws of physics involved in riding a bike, yet you are usually able to move forward and stay upright. Riding a bicycle is an example of being unaware of conscious actions and relying on unconscious muscle memory that you use to achieve a result.

An example of an application of unconscious mind is illustrated when we lift an object from the floor and all of our muscles must be coordinated and orchestrated to complete the task. However, the unconscious brain is not of interest in this book. Our conscious brain is aware of some activities and mostly unaware of others. Whether conscious or unconscious, the information that the brain senses is processed into our memory. These imprinted memories serve to create filters that have both explicit and implicit bias and act to interpret the world for each of us. Here's the punch line, no two people have the same perceived world-view. There are simply too many variables.

You observe something, automatically run it through your filters and assign meaning and formulate an expected result. It's only when the results are different than you anticipated that you become aware of this process. It's fair to postulate that the likelihood of two people having the same filters is less likely than the odds of winning the Powerball lottery jackpot.

Books on negotiation tend to fixate on behaviors and subsequent results. *Stop Blaming the Fish* travels further upstream. It deals with how you perceive situations and then set expectations and drive the rest of the cycle. Without having a holistic view of this process, people get stuck in an activity trap without regard for what's happening, sort of a rote stimulus-response loop; act and get results, act and get results, act and get results, etc. This approach can only lead to long-term failure. Eventually, you will find that acting does not produce the desired result. You need to understand how your perceptions, expectations, and behaviors interact to create results before you can examine how personality traits impact negotiations. Coupled with the results of the Global Five, understanding the cause and effect relationship of the negotiating cycle and the negotiating spectrum will enable you to better understand and predict more accurately how you will perform in an uncertain negotiating situation. Predictive models are just that and prone to error. The more subjective you are when approaching negotiating, the higher the propensity for mistakes.

The Negotiating Cycle

Here's how each element interacts and relates to negotiations starting at the end with **Results**. Results are a manifestation of our decisions and actions. **Behaviors** are the actions and reactions taken when communicating with another. Included are the concessions, demands, ploys, tactics, and information you use in the process, as well as unconscious actions. **Expectations** are what you believe is achievable given a particular set of circumstances. They drive our behaviors. **Perceptions** are the set of stored filters created by your location that you use to process, sort and judge situations and information you encounter. Based on our understanding you will develop an expectation of results for any given situation. This process is not limited to negotiation but is fundamentally the way you navigate life. So, where do these perceptions originate?

The actions or behaviors that you experience in interactions with another person serve to either confirm or refute your **perceptions** of reality. Based on these perceptions, your reality is either reinforced or discredited. If reinforced, you tend to dig in and feel reassured. If refuted, you tend to spiral out of control temporarily, become confused and start searching for a new reality. Here's how perceptions, expectations, behaviors and results relate. You enter the negotiating arena with expectations of results based on your perceptions. You observe behavior in a negotiation, interpret it, and that either reinforces or alters your perceptions. If your perceptions are confirmed, it strengthens your expectations and drives your behavior toward the expected end. If it does not confirm your impressions, then confusion occurs, and expectations are adjusted. This adjustment, either up or down, drives your behavior, which impacts the results.

Perceptions drive expectations and expectations drive behavior, action or performance. Consider the Rosenthal effect--the phenomenon whereby higher expectations lead to an increase in performance. Robert Rosenthal and Lenore Jacobson conducted a classroom study that showed that when a teacher raised expectations of performance among their students, the students achieved higher scores. This shows that the expectations of others can influence your performance and that the higher the expectation the better the result or conversely, the lower the expectation, the lower the results. Remember, perceptions, influenced by your location, drive expectations. Perceptions create expectations that drive behavior that in turn create results. Results also either reinforce or challenge expectations. And the wheel goes round and round.

The practice of negotiation is not about the business of manipulating, exploiting, persuading, proving, convincing, leveraging power or hard bargaining, although they are part of most skilled negotiator's arsenal of weapons. It's more about expectation engineering. Expectation setting is theoretical, while engineering is the practice of applying theory to life. A great negotiator is great at perception and expectation engineering and, in most cases, re-engineering.

The primary purpose of this book is to have you understand that to be an effective negotiator, you must know yourself. That is the basis of your perceptions, how you tend to set expectations and how they drive your behavior and ultimately the results. Perceptions are always multifaceted.

Negotiating Spectrum

A "one size fits all" approach to negotiation is not a sustainable strategy and usually fails miserably. Is your exemplar the master negotiator, who absolutely is the best at bargaining and getting his way in a deal? Or is your role model a self-sacrificing benefactor, who gives unselfishly? I firmly believe that both of these extremes are myopic, because they deal with only one side of the equation.

The graphic that follows illustrates the components that are crucial to an expanded definition of negotiations. I call this framework the Negotiating Spectrum. The spectrum expands upon the work of Adam Grant, a professor at The Wharton School at the University of Pennsylvania, which he presented in his book *Give and Take*. Grant defines how different styles of networking, collaboration, influence, negotiation, and leadership interact. The purpose of what follows is to portray the relationship of negotiating styles as a self-diagnostic to take stock and assist you in better understanding yourself and others. The spectrum will serve as a touchstone. Where do you reside on the spectrum?

As mentioned, the Negotiating Spectrum defines your negotiating style along continuums in terms of the dimensions of strategy, tactics, defaults, adaptability, empathy, propensity to find opportunities to negotiate, and perspective on availability of resources. Continuums rarely present themselves as black and white or absolutes. Rather they are revealed as varying shades of gray. If you are unfamiliar with these terms or want to review them in more depth please refer to the Tackle Box section at the end of this book where they are defined and fully explained. For now, you should focus on Negotiating Styles.

Negotiating Style:	Selfless Givers	Strategic Givers	Matchers	Takers	Social Darwinists
Strategy:	Avoid Conflict	Pay-it-forward	Quid pro quo	Defeat	Crush
Tactics:	Appease	Accede Collaborate Compromise	Collaborate Persuade Influence Compromise Bargain Power Play Coerce	Bargain Power Play Coerce	Power Play Coerce
Default:	Relationship				Gain
Adaptability:	Accommodat				Egocentric
Empathy:	Too Much				None
Propensity to Find Opportunities to Negotiate	Avoid				Find
Perspective on Availabilty of Resources	Plenty				Scarcity

Negotiating Spectrum

Adam Grant's *Give & Take* provided the basis for negotiating styles. Grant classifies people's styles as Givers, Matchers or Takers. I have expanded the classifications to include Social Darwinists at one extreme of the continuum and Selfless and Strategic Givers, a twist on Givers, at the other. I offer a word of warning about negotiating style; the primary driver is not behavior, it's intent. Regrettably, just because you see the behavior does not mean you see the purpose. In addition to understanding, careful observation and thoughtful questioning are the best vehicles to determine intent. The factor that contributes most significantly to negotiating style is the degree to which you accommodate. For clarity, here are illustrations of each of the five negotiating style.

The **Selfless Giver** will give you the shirt off of their back without regard to how they will benefit. I am not addressing people who are purposely working toward a higher goal or power in this category. The people I reference here are extremely uncomfortable with conflict of any kind. They are easy to exploit and regularly preyed upon. Being a nice person is not a defensive strategy. They avoid conflict through appeasement. They invariably will default to the Relationship at the expense of Gain. They have an extremely high propensity to accommodate others at their expense. Empathy is the grease that keeps their giving factory running. They may be empathetic to a fault. Emotion primarily drives Selfless Givers rather than rationality. They negotiate by not engaging in the process, and purposely avoid it. We all know someone who fits this description. They are an easy mark for anyone up the food chain; that is, anyone who's default is Gain instead of Relationship.

Strategic Givers are givers with a real purpose. They come from a mindset of abundance rather than scarcity. They expect to reap benefits or garner gain by paying-it-forward, albeit maybe not directly for themselves. The returns to this style may be to serve the greater good of humanity or to further their agenda. Strategic Givers may or may not be philanthropic, but they do help others to succeed through advice, networking, connections, opportunities and capital. They employ the behaviors of acceding (granting favors), collaborating and compromise. To be clear, a strategic giver is not a pushover like the selfless giver. These are usually people that have a keen eye toward helping others who deserve and appreciate being helped. Favors may not be given to everyone in equal proportions. Long-term gain is clearly the focus.

An example of a Strategic Giver was Milton Hershey, the American confectioner, and philanthropist. He founded the Hershey Chocolate Company, eventually becoming exceedingly successful. As he and his wife had no children, they turned to philanthropy and established the Hershey Industrial School. Hershey transferred the majority of his assets, including control of the company, to the Milton Hershey School Trust Fund, to benefit the Industrial School. Another example of his strategic giving was building the grand Hotel Hershey during the height of Great Depression solely to keep his workers employed and their family's fed. Hershey gave his money to help many others, but his selflessness was dependent on the desire to establish his legacy as a successful and compassionate business owner.

Here is a word of warning. If Strategic Givers are exploited or deceived by those they try to help, they can quickly turn bitter. They exhibit empathy to those who appreciate and respect their contributions.

The ***Matcher*** defines the mean of the negotiating bell curve. Matchers like all other styles are not homogeneous; they're a very mixed bag. Their expectation is to trade *quid pro quo* (Latin for "something for something," or "one thing for another") so that their interests and needs are met. Matchers strive for agreement but do not necessarily always try to balance Relationship and Gain. They use a wide variety of behaviors to achieve their goals including; collaboration, persuasion, influence, compromise, bargaining, power tactics and even coercion in varying degrees.

All Matchers are consciously or unconsciously aware of keeping score and of the need to keep Relationship and Gain at different levels of balance. They tend not to be on the extremes of the Accommodate/Egocentric continuum. They exhibit varying levels of empathy from high to low, but it is palpable. Matching as a negotiating strategy is pervasive in business and politics. Examples include labor relations contracts, agreements for raw materials or components, employment agreements, purchase agreements, treaties, software licenses, service agreements, trade agreements, and prenuptial agreements. The value of the goods, services or item of consideration is exchanged for another consideration, like money, equity, and alike. Often, people whose primary style is matching default to viewing negotiations as a zero-sum game. That is the mathematical representation of a negotiation in which each participant's gain (or loss) of value is precisely balanced by the losses (or gains) of the value of others participant. A zero sum game is referred to as 'fixed pie.'

The fixed pie syndrome is one of those bizarre anomalies that still persist surreptitiously in the cultures of many organizations. There are times that the pie is definitely fixed, but to approach each negotiation from this perspective is myopic. The fixed pie syndrome is a rigid mindset. The practitioner sees nothing more than what sits on the negotiation table. Many agreements fail to materialize because of this limited vision. The resulting loss of possibilities and potential trade-offs forces the opposing parties to squabble over a single issue while dozens more lay scattered about them. They are all opportunities that are missed. The following case study, courtesy of www.negotiations.com exemplifies the pitfalls of assuming a fixed pie when employing matching as a strategy.

"In late 1985, Frank Borman, the former renowned astronaut, was the acting president of Eastern Airlines, based in the U.S. The airline was struggling through tough and trying economic times. Labor costs were a critical issue that Mr. Borman sought to address. Imperiously, Mr. Borman tossed an ultimatum at the three unions like a gauntlet. Either they were to agree to give the airline substantial wage concessions or he would sell the airline. The union leaders were not impressed by the threat as they all had binding contracts that were not to be renegotiated for some time to come. They believed that the threat to sell off the airline had a hollow ring to it and called what they perceived to be a bluff. To add weight to his edict, Mr. Borman began to initiate talks with Frank Lorenzo, also known as Frankie Smooth Talk, an industry heavyweight who had previously crushed the unions at Continental Airlines. Lorenzo was known to be ruthless. Borman's talking with Lorenzo apparently made the union jittery. What the unions didn't know was that Borman was bluffing, as he didn't intend to sell the airline."

"Lorenzo however, and not aware of Borman's slight of hand tactics, submitted such a significant proposal to the Board of Directors of Eastern Airlines, they began to seriously look at the offer with raised eyebrows and considerable interest. The unions, in the meantime, began to rethink their position. As the negotiations progressed, Borman began to make some grudging, but significant headway with his negotiations with two of the three unions. Both the flight attendants' and pilots' unions agreed to a 20 percent wage give back."

"However, the machinists' unions, which were run by the hard-nosed Charlie Bryan, would only agree to a 15 percent slash in wages. Borman didn't accept their position. They argued voraciously over the dispute five percent, and both of them took the position that if either side were to fail to make a concession over the disputed amount, the airline would be ruined."

"Like two drivers aiming head on at each other, eyes fixated and jaws squared, they steeled themselves, waiting for who would blink first. Neither did, and they crashed headlong into each other, stubborn to the end as the looming deadline for Lorenzo's offer arrived. The Board of Directors for Eastern Airlines accepted Lorenzo's offer. As a result, Borman was tossed, and out of a job. To the bitter end that followed, Lorenzo forced massive wage cuts on the hapless unions and eliminated so many jobs that Eastern Airlines was soon to go the way of the Dodo bird – just another extinct species. It filed for bankruptcy in March of 1989."

Winning is paramount for **Takers**. They strive to defeat others by using power plays and other forms of leverage exploitation as their primary behaviors. They will invariably work to serve their self-interests. They will exploit other less dominant ways to reach closure and secure what they need if their perceived power is eroded. Gain is their main motivation, but Takers recognize the need to maintain a Relationship in some situations. Takers tend to gravitate toward the Egocentric pole of the Adaptability scale and usually exhibit some, but little empathy.

Takers tend to be hyper-rational and totally selfish. In economic terms they embody the characteristics of ultimate rationalist homo economicus. Homo economicus, economic man, or Econs, is a concept within economic theory depicting humans as being consistently rational and narrowly self-interested intermediates who usually pursue their defined ends optimally. Econs can make any calculation perfectly accurately, have no self-control problems, are not over-confident and makes accurate forecasts. So do Econs display emotions or feelings? According to Richard Thaler, Professor of Economics and Behavioral Science at University of Chicago's Booth School, "Well, *homo economicus* doesn't much pay attention to social norms, unless it's gonna hurt them financially." Econs are true Takers and commit to a goal of optimizing their position and working in their best interest including adhering to social norms of demonstrating humanoid emotions. They use an evaluation model of cost, benefit, probability and risk to determine if doing something is in line with their goal.

To illustrate, Takers are the consummate free riders. Free riders are defined as non-paying consumers who cannot resist using something that is offered for free if it does not reduce the amount available for others. For example, free riding is when people refuse to voluntarily pay or tip, for a public good or service such as a street musician. There is no charge for the musician's service, but tipping is expected if the service is appreciated. Takers will not tip because of the free riding belief that tipping is not in their economic best interest. As Star Trek's Spock would say, "It's only logical." A true homo economicus is very rare, but they do exist. More people than you think tend to strongly gravitate to the self-serving, personal optimization philosophy. They are Takers and invariably put their self-interests first.

Steve Jobs might be construed as a Taker. His persona exuded a rigid, "my way or the highway" mindset. This is not a condemnation of Jobs but a look at what type of individual it took to create Apple, revolutionize at least four industries and to take on Microsoft head-to-head. A relentless, demanding, impatient perfectionist, Jobs had the reputation of being a hot-tempered manager throughout his life. In 1987, the New York Times wrote: "by the early 80's, Mr. Jobs was widely hated at Apple. Senior management had to endure his temper tantrums. He created resentment among employees by turning some into stars and insulting others, often reducing them to tears. Mr. Jobs himself would frequently cry after fights with fellow executives." Jobs did have the capacity for feelings and empathy, but his drive for excellence relegated relationships to a distant second place. Twenty years later, after reclaiming the helm at Apple, Jobs was little different. There was still the mercurialness--the tantrums, hours-long, dictator-like speeches, the famous, desperate, and transparent hogging of credit. But he also became more of a charismatic leader, and more complex.

A **Social Darwinist** is a "Taker" on steroids. They exemplify this quotation from Mark Twain, "Of all the animals, man is the only one that is cruel." The underlying supposition is that for me to win I have to make you lose. Social Darwinism, a term coined in the late 19th century to describe the idea that humans, like animals and plants, compete in a struggle for existence in which natural selection results in "survival of the fittest." Herbert Spencer, who coined the term, was an enormously influential English philosopher and agnostic of the

Victorian era. Social Darwinism is a name given to various theories of society which emerged in the United Kingdom, North America, and Western Europe in the 1870s, and which claim to apply biological concepts of natural selection and survival of the fittest to sociology and politics.

Social Darwinists in the business world are snakes in suits. Their expectation is not merely to defeat but to completely crush their adversary. Their instruction manual is Robert Greene's *48 Laws of Power*. They rely on power tactics to exploit their leverage and take advantage of the weakness of others. Relationship has no value, and they are incapable of exhibiting genuine empathy. These people are rare, but avoid any negotiations with them because they are borderline sociopaths. Appealing to their better self is ineffective. They are incapable of relating to other people's pain, because they are devoid of empathy.

John A. Byrne chronicles a Social Darwinist in his book *Chainsaw* about "Chainsaw Al" Dunlap. When Dunlap was CEO of Scott Paper in the 1990s, he sold the company to Kimberly-Clark for $7.8 billion and walked away with $100 million in bonuses. Shortly after leaving Scott Paper, he took over as chairman and CEO of Sunbeam, which subsequently reported record earnings the next year. Dunlap attempted to replicate the Scott Paper sale, but was unable to find a buyer so he decided instead to buy a controlling interest in Coleman, Signature Brands and First Alert. Within days, Sunbeam's stock jumped to an all-time high.

Dunlap's strategy inflated revenues and led the board to review Dunlap's performance. The board found that Dunlap had sold retailers far more merchandise than they could handle. With the stores hopelessly overstocked, unsold inventory piled up in Sunbeam's warehouses. As a result, Sunbeam faced losses of as much as $60 million in the second quarter of 1998. Dunlap had told the company controller to push the limits of accounting principles. In June 1998, Dunlap was fired. The shareholder suit against Dunlap dragged on until 2002, when he agreed to pay $15 million to settle the allegations.

The Securities and Exchange Commission (SEC) sued Dunlap, alleging that he had engineered a massive accounting fraud. An SEC investigation revealed that Dunlap had created the impression of a greater loss the year he assumed leadership of Sunbeam in order to make it look like the company had experienced a dramatic turnaround. The SEC estimated that at least $60 million of Sunbeam's earnings in 1997 were fraudulent. He also offered incentives for retailers to sell products that would have otherwise been sold later in the year, a practice known as "channel stuffing." The SEC also argued that the purchases of Coleman, Signature and First Alert were made to conceal Sunbeam's growing financial problems. By that time it was too late and Sunbeam was unable to recover and was forced into bankruptcy in 2002. Dunlap was also suspected of irregularities while at Scott Paper.

Like most CEOs, Dunlap believed that the primary goal of any business should be to make money for its shareholders. He believed in making widespread cuts, and massive layoffs to streamline operations by firing thousands of employees at once and closing multiple plants and factories. According to Jon Ronson, author of the Psychopath Test, Dunlap fired people with such apparent glee that Fast Company, a business magazine, included him in an article about potential psychopathic CEOs. He drastically changed the economic might of such corporations as Scott Paper and Sunbeam without a modicum of empathy for the shareholders, employees or customers. Dunlap sure sounds like a Social Darwinist to me, but he is not alone. Jack Welch, the revered former CEO of GE, was given the name Neutron Jack because, like a neutron bomb after detonation, Welch wiped out employees, but not the buildings. Perhaps this psychological profile applies to a certain deal making entrepreneur turned politician as well, but I'll let you be the judge.

So is being a Social Darwinist a bad strategy? After all Dunlap and others have amassed great fortunes from these behaviors. I'll let you decide. Here's some food for thought. William Muir is an evolutionary biologist at Purdue University who studied chicken productivity. The measure of productivity for chickens is simple--just count the eggs they lay. He researched ways to make chickens more productive by devising a rather ingenious experiment. Since chickens live in groups, he selected an average flock as his control and left it alone laying eggs and living intact for six generations. He created a second group of the individually most productive chickens. He placed these "super chickens" into a "superflock." In each successive generation, he selected only the most productive for breeding.

After six generations he compared the results of the control group to those of the superflock. The control group was doing just fine. They were all plump and fully feathered and egg production had increased notably. That wasn't surprising, but what happened to the superflock was. All but three of the flocks were dead. They'd pecked each other to death. The individually productive chickens had only achieved their success by suppressing the productivity of the rest.

The super chicken model is what drives the Social Darwinist, picking the superstars, the brightest men, or occasionally women, in the room, and giving them all the resources and all the power to achieve success. And the results tend to be the same as in William Muir's experiment: aggression, dysfunction, and waste. The only way to be successful is by suppressing the rest, or a strategy of 'for me to win, you have to lose.'

Stupid Stuff That People Do as a Substitute for Logical Thinking

"What a piece of work is a man, how noble in reason, how infinite in faculties, in form and moving how express and admirable, in action how like an angel, in apprehension how like a god."

William Shakespeare

Shakespeare's Hamlet is not praising man, but being cynical and saying while humans may appear to think and act "nobly" they are really essentially less than honorable. He is expressing his despondency over the difference between the best that men aspire to be, and how they actually behave. If man's intent is to be moral, logical, worthy and benevolent, then what causes him not to be that? The fact is that the human brain does not consistently or reliably produce logical results. The brain is attached to a person and subject to emotions, feelings, subjectivity and flawed thinking. For now, let's stay with the brain has a proclivity to not always produce logical interpretations, judgments, decisions and actions.

Fallacies are common errors in reasoning that will undermine the logic of your argument. Flaws in your thinking render many of your judgments, interpretations and decisions irrational. Fallacies can be either illegitimate arguments or irrelevant points. They are fallacies because they lack evidence that supports their claim. They have a compound effect in that neither the person using the fallacious argument nor the person receiving it is usually aware of it being faulty. Illegitimate arguments are based upon flawed logic, where irrelevant points do not fit the point being argued. They are surprisingly more pervasive in usage than you might think. I'll share some common examples later.

The problem is that most of us don't realize that we are being illogical or irrelevant. So what causes this to happen? The answer lies in how the mind uses metaphors and heuristics to judging, interpreting, problem solving and decision-making. Metaphors and heuristics help form the cognitive insular "bubble" in which we all exist. "Metaphors for most people are a tool of the lyrical imagination and the rhetorical embellishment, using extraordinary rather than common language. George P. Lakoff, an American cognitive linguist, offer a thesis that individuals are significantly influenced by the central metaphors they use to explain complex phenomena. In *Metaphors We Live By*, Lakoff says the truth is that metaphors are pervasive in everyday life, not just in language but also in thought and action. The concepts that guide our thought and actions are not just matters of the mind. They also direct our everyday functioning, down to the most basic details. Our concepts organize what we perceive, how we get around in the world, and how we relate to other people. The way we think, what we experience and what we do every day is largely metaphorical in nature. Metaphors not only make our thoughts more vivid and interesting but that they actually structure our perceptions and understanding. There is a danger in relying too heavily on metaphors to understand the world around us because they are often simplistic and a forced fit.

Heuristics are a practical method not guaranteed to be optimal or exact. If finding an optimal solution is impossible, complex or impractical in the conduct of everyday life, then heuristic methods seem elegant to speed up the process of finding a satisfactory solution. Heuristic methods include using rules of thumb, educated guesses, intuitive judgments, stereotyping, profiling, or common sense.

Heuristics, which are used in judgment and decision-making, are simple, efficient rules. People tend to use them excessively to form judgments and make decisions to avoid cognitive overload. These mental shortcuts usually involve focusing on one aspect of a complex problem and ignoring others. Regrettably, the people who are the recipients of these flawed arguments use the same heuristic processes and fall into the same trap.

These highly economical and usually effective heuristics can lead to systematic and predictable errors because they are illogical. They trade rationality (certainty) for intuitiveness (speed). The unstated premise here is that people make emotional decisions for what they perceive as logical reasons. A better understanding of these heuristics and of the biases to which they lead could improve judgments and decisions in situations of uncertainty. Although efficient, using them unconsciously could lead to bad judgments and decision subsequently rendering devastating results.

In 1973, Amos Tversky and Daniel Kahneman, who where initially both professors of psychology at Hebrew University, published *Judgment Under Uncertainty: Heuristics And Biases*, which identified three common heuristics or rules of thumb that people employ. They were; representativeness, availability and anchoring. Since the outcome of negotiation are variable and have a degree of uncertainty these rules of thumb have great utility. Below is a discussion on the application and implications to negotiating for each rule of thumb. Subsequently, Kahneman became a Nobel laureate in Economics. His groundbreaking work focused on the new field of behavioral economics.

Representativeness is a mental shortcut used when making judgments about the probability of an event under uncertainty. Or, judging a situation based on how similar the subjects are to the models the person holds in his or her mind. If the situation loosely fits the model the model defines the situation or event. Using very little data, a pattern is derived that fits a stored mental model and decisions are made intuitively. This situation resembles a previous experience and dictates the answer.

Let's say that you are negotiating with someone that you have not worked with in the past. You make your opening offer, which has ample room to negotiate. The person across the table can then accept, make a counter offer or reject it. Depending on their response you will have a deal, accept a counter offer, make a counter to their counter offer or reject it. That is how representativeness works in negotiations. Your responses are preprogrammed based upon what you have seen in the past. It's an 'if ... then' algorithm that is stored in the brain. If X happens it means Y and then you react accordingly. This is the realm of tactics in negotiations. Based upon your negotiating experience you decode the cues that your counterpart sends and respond accordingly.

Availability is a mental shortcut that occurs when people make judgments about the probability of events based on the ease with which examples come to mind. For example during a Tversky & Kahneman experiment, the majority of participants reported that there were more words in the English language that start with the letter K than for which K was the third letter. There are actually twice as many words in the English Language that have K as the third letter as those that start with K, but words that start with K are much easier to recall and bring to mind. Top of mind recall can also occur because of something that has recently happened, was memorable or was particularly vivid.

This rule of thumb manifests itself in negotiations through your default negotiating style and the negotiating cycle. You will be extra sensitive to cues, words and tactics that trigger your tendency toward Relationship and Gain because they are top of mind. Your world-view will impact your expectations even before the negotiations begin. Availability if left unchecked will expose whom you are. It can be altered through learned behaviors as a defense mechanism.

Anchoring is the common human tendency to rely too heavily on the first piece of information offered (the "anchor") when making decisions. For example, in a study done with university students, groups were told to quickly solve a problem. One group had to calculate 1x2x3x4x5x6x7x8 while the other group had to solve 8x7x6x5x4x3x2x1. The experiment was repeated so that the results were statistically valid. Groups that were given a high "base" number (anchor) of eight, as in 8x7x6x5x4x3x2x1, overwhelmingly estimated the product more accurately. Conversely, the groups with the lower base, or anchor, number of one estimated the answer to be significantly lower. The actual answer of either calculation is 40,320.

The way anchoring plays out in negotiations is deceptively simple but insidious. Opening offers or positions are rarely where negotiations wind up. We are conditioned to believe that people always leave some room to negotiate when they make their initial demands. The question is how much negotiating room is there? Opening offers tend to affect expectations of an outcome. If you are on the receiving end then a low offer will cause you to think that you have lots of work to do to get the settlement you want and shifts leverage to your counterpart. A high offer will tend to encourage you to ask for even more and gives you leverage. Anchoring also sets the floor and the ceiling of the negotiation. The area in the middle between the floor and the ceiling becomes the negotiating space.

Tversky & Kahneman's work on **Aversion to Loss** and **Framing** and their implications to negotiating bear mention as well. The **Aversion to Loss** principle offers insight to how people value gains and risk. In economics and decision theory, loss aversion refers to people's tendency to strongly prefer avoiding losses to acquiring gains. Most studies suggest that losses are twice as powerful, psychologically, as gains. This infers that it's easier to negotiate with someone who has something at risk than someone who does not.

Framing suggests that decisions can be made easier based upon the way the story is presented. People love and can relate to stories. Storytelling plays an important role in the human reasoning processes and in helping convince others. When persuading others, the people preferred stories to abstract arguments, demands or statistical measures. When situations are complex, like negotiations, narrative allows the people to involve more of the context versus the content. Make no mistake; in negotiations storytelling and framing are usually purposeful and planned. The story is wrapped around a goal. The delivery is intentional and can be deceptive.

Moving beyond Tversky & Kahneman's body of work there are three other common heuristics that also have utility in negotiations. The first is **naïve diversification,** the theory that people tend to diversify more when asked to make several choices at once than when making the same type of decision sequentially. This happens because people attempt to hedge their bets and avoid the risk of losing more when dealing with an uncertain future and having to make judgments about the future with limited knowledge. In long-term negotiations where there are complex issues that must be decided at the beginning of an agreement, negotiators will tend to anticipate situations and remedies that have little to no likelihood of occurrence, "just in case." Naïve diversification is not wrong, but if you are involved in a complex business agreement, partnership, negotiating a prenuptial agreement or divorce settlement, then be prepare to encounter this phenomenon. If children are involve in a divorce settlement the complexity, acrimony and angst becomes exponential.

Escalation of commitment is the phenomenon where people justify increased investment in a decision based on the cumulative prior investment. They dig in their heals and despite a preponderance of new evidence suggesting that today's cost of continuing the decision outweighs the expected benefit continue to pursue the goal. In negotiations making people work for any gain will tend to increase their commitment to concluding out a deal. I call this phenomenon sweat equity. The more people work for something the more they become committed to accomplishing it despite dealing with the law of diminishing returns. Self-inflicted pressure causes a tendency to make unplanned, major concessions increases, to close the deal.

Familiarity is another mental shortcut applied to various situations in which individuals assume that the circumstances underlying the past behavior still hold true for the present situation and that the past behavior thus can be correctly applied to the new situation. It plays to the human desire of constancy and permanence. It is the reason why people tend to do business with those they know and trust. Interestingly, many of these business relationships produce unsatisfactory results impacting not only Gain but the Relationship as well.

In negotiations, over familiarity can be synonymous for predictability. Unpredictability can throw a situation out of balance and create confusion and uncertainty. In a long term, high stakes, high relationship situation, like a marriage or business relationship being consistent and mostly predictable is essential, but being unpredictable and inconsistent can be disastrous. In a short term, high gain and low relationship environment being unpredictable and inconsistent can provide strategic leverage. The element of surprise is desirable in more positional situations like; military battles, one-time negotiations on high-ticket items.

Thus far we talked about how the mind uses metaphors and heuristics to judge and decide, but as a negotiator be on the look out for **common fallacies** that people try to present as a substitute for logic. You might be an unconscious offender. Many tactics used in negotiating are based upon these fallacies. A complete list of these logical fallacies is included in the Tackle Box section of this book. Here's an example of a common fallacy of logic. **Stereotyping** is form of the hasty generalization fallacy. It happens, for example, when someone says, "All Asian's are tough negotiators." Such a sweeping claim about all members of a particular ethnic, religious, racial, or political group is stereotyping. Yet another kind of stereotyping is sexism, which occurs when someone discriminates against another person based on gender. For example, when an observer a negotiation involving a women and a man, if a person makes a comment about "men are much better negotiators than women," the person is guilty of a combination of stereotyping and sexism—both components of hasty generalization.

Chapter IV - How To Improve Your Catch

"Don't fight a battle if you don't gain anything by winning."

Field Marshall Erwin Rommel

Sport fishing is controlled by catch limits and seasons. Quantity, time and size are regulated to keep the fish population at healthy, sustainable levels. Negotiation may be thought of in a similar way, but in this case, limits are self-regulated. There will always be those who are greedy and will always scheme to exceed the limits, like an indiscriminate hunter who subscribes to the axiom, "if it flies it dies." The following is not intended for their consumption.

This next section offers strategies for acknowledging your personality defaults, challenging your perceptions, managing your expectations and changing your behavior, all to improve your negotiating results. The strategies range from general to specific. First, I'll share a few overarching Master Strategies that form the philosophical basis of improvement for everyone. Then, I'll present Macro Strategies that everyone has at their disposal when negotiating. Lastly, I'll offer prescriptive Micro Strategies to assist in shifting the balance between Gain and Relationship. There are two sets of Micro Strategies. Each is specifically targeted to different audiences; those who default to trading Gain for Relationship and those who have the reciprocal default.

Master Strategies
Own your stuff – Your perceptions, location, and defaults were all formulated in the past. They are persistent. They do not change readily. To improve future results you need to work backward through the cycle of events. If you want to change results, then you need to change behavior. Behavior is driven by expectations of a situation, which are formulated by the way you perceive the world, or your location. Your perceptions are unconsciously driving you. Other than a significant emotional event, behavior science broadly agrees that your perceptions are formulated and are pretty locked-in during adolescence. You need to get control of what and how you perceive, i.e. the filters and lenses you use to interpret and navigate the world.

Through awareness, understanding, and mindfulness you can manage these perceptions and not be controlled by them. They will still be there, but consciously. For example, having the understanding that you have extreme defaults such as high or low accommodation proclivity is a great first step. Knowing that your first inclination is to create harmony and balance with the rest of the world is noble, but is always at your expense. Or, you may recognize that you have gained extreme material wealth at the expense of everyone else. Awareness is incredible but utterly useless unless acted upon. Ownership comes from having both the acknowledgment and commitment to change.

Take the long view – Negotiating is not a sport. It is a way to resolve issues temporarily among people or groups of people. A successful negotiation does not have to yield equal results. It does, however, need to provide all parties with what they need without irreparable damage to the relationship. Again the balance and tension between Gain and Relationship is essential to success.

Regrettably, some of us unwittingly assume that negotiations are completed in a vacuum and that it's all about winning. Those who assume that winning is free and without consequence see only the Gain side of the equation. Others extract themselves from the negotiating arena by defaulting to Relationship at their expense. Both strategies are problematic and myopic.

Look for the common ground – Negotiation is a viable problem resolution process only if there is at least a modicum of common ground. If absolutism dominates the issues because the problem is steeped in morality and beliefs, then it is a classical example with no common ground, no room for compromise or give and take. It is deadlocked from the onset. Avoid issues that have a moral impasse implicit, or driven by ideology, or have too many moving parts, or have already been resolved. They are outside of the domain of negotiations.

Macro Strategies
Regardless of your default settings or preferences in negotiations, there are four macro strategies that are always at your disposal. You can accept, deal with, defer or ignore a particular issue, proposal, claim, threat or piece of information: You can **accept** what has been raised and move on, **defer** what has been said and table the issue with the

consent of others, ***ignore*** it as if it had not occurred, or ***deal with*** the issue by engaging in substantive dialogue. To keep others involved in the process always legitimize what they say, feel or are concerned about. You don't need to agree with them, you just need to acknowledge that they were heard.

Accept: The process of accepting an issue is self-explanatory. Dealing with an issue may impede planned progress because it takes time and effort. If the issue is important to both parties and attempts at deferral may not be successful, then you will need to deal with the issue or risk that it will resurface later in the negotiation or, worse, derail it completely.

Defer: Deferring can be used in at least two ways. The first is a distraction to move on, or as a genuine attempt to postpone dealing with the issue later. There is a risk if you try to avoid dealing with an issue by deferring it. If you are caught making a pivot deferring the issue that was raised, then you run the risk of being perceived as less than honest. Remember, final agreements are usually a consequence of reaching multiple smaller, sometimes superficially insignificant ones. Deferring an issue is, in fact, an implicit agreement to revisit it.

Ignore: The last option a negotiator has when an issue is raised is ignoring it. Pretend that it was never mentioned. This strategy can be very effective since in the course of a negotiation comments are made simply to solicit a response or reaction. They are used to test the other person. If you perceive that someone is engaging in that practice then ignoring may be a viable option. If it is raised again, then asking 'are you serious?' might help. If they are not, your options are to accept, deal with or defer the issue. Ignoring can be a risk strategy since it may impact the relationship. Conversely, dealing with every issue that is raised during a negotiation may land you in a black hole.

Deal with: You must deal with and issue if accepting, deferring and ignoring are not acceptable remedies, or the issue at hand is hindering resolution of a larger problem. Dealing with an issue can be risky. You may jump into a situation without being fully prepared. It can also consume valuable time and potentially derail the negotiating process. The advantage of dealing with an issue as it arises is that if successfully resolved it can greatly accelerate progress and build trust.

To stay on the same page, you must address genuine issues as they arise. They come in three types; misunderstandings, doubt and perceived shortcomings. Let's discuss how to properly and effectively respond using an if/then response scenario.

If the person with whom you are dealing is raising an issue or objecting because they misunderstand what you are saying, then you must clarify so that the person receiving your message understands what you intend. If a real problem is being raised, such as the wrong price on an invoice, late delivery on previous orders, a defective product received or poor service experienced, then the appropriate response is to show action to remedy the situation. Too often, I have personally experienced totally wrong responses to this issue. Offering an apology or an excuse falls far short of addressing the issue. An action is required. If others are expressing doubt, skepticism or disbelief of what you are offering, then proof or evidence is required to remove that barrier to progress. Lastly, if others are raising an issue that they perceive as a shortcoming, then ensure that there is not a misunderstanding. Think about it. Ignoring or deferring a significant issue will grind progress to a full stop. These are showstoppers. If not addressed appropriately, they can severely impact the results of the discussion and the problem resolution process. Let's take each of the issues and discuss how to offer an appropriate response.

Issue: *Misunderstanding*
<u>Response:</u> Clarify what you were trying to say.
This disconnect can be incredibly frustrating because the issue might be that there is a bona fide misunderstanding or that others are playing dumb. To clarify a misunderstanding, you need to assess if others don't understand or are only using the tactic of playing dumb to gain additional information. Attempt to restate, not repeat, what you previously offered without sharing additional information. Take responsibility for the miscommunication and rephrase the statement to more clearly communicate it. If the misunderstanding is not clarified in three or four attempts, ask them, "what seems to be at the root of the disconnect?" Once you think that you have adequately clarified the issue, then check with others to confirm that you have indeed cleared the misunderstanding before proceeding to the next step.

Unlike misunderstandings, real problems are not resolved by explaining. You need to act to resolve the issues. Real problems may take the form of performance issues or capability deficiencies. As an example, a manufacturer that has plans to grow beyond its existing service footprint may not consider distributors that do not have service capabilities in the new expansion territory. Even though your distribution company might have served the manufacturer well, your lack of capability in that geography presents a real problem for the manufacturer. To resolve the issue, you might have to develop a plan to grow your capability service to that new geography. Performance issues such as product/service quality, timeliness, and accuracy of documentation must be resolved before going to the next step to stay in sync with others.

A standard objection faced by sellers is the often-heard argument that your price is too high. Again, you face the quintessential question, are these ploys simply to get you to lower your price or are they real problems? The easy way out for a seller is to treat the objection as a real problem and drop their price--but does that action resolve the issue? You need to peel back the onion to get to the core or root of the objection. Price may only be the symptom or a tactic designed to test if there is any fat in the seller's offer. The real problem may be that our product/service is over designed for the applications. That's a fit or offering issue, not a price issue. Free advice: always get to the heart of the matter before making a concession.

Issue: Doubt or skepticism
Response: Show proof or evidence that your statement or claim is valid. Be careful not to offer too much or submit proof that does not resonate with others. Before offering evidence, have others commit to defining what proof or evidence would satisfy their doubt.

Issue: Perceived shortcoming.
Response: This is the most difficult to deal with because perception is between someone's ears. If someone believes something to be true, by definition it is true. Arguing whether something is true may not move the conversation forward. If you cannot address the misconception by clarifying, then use the Company Song--a series of messages that relays the same idea in a different way. The message will always be consistent, but the words may be different. When faced with someone

that sees your offering as having a perceived shortcoming, first try to clarify the issue so that they realize their perception may not be accurate. Failing that strategy, step back and present the Company Song as a way to minimize the impact of that erroneous perception first, determine the nature of the objection or issue being raised by others. Next, confirm what you are hearing and the nature of what they are saying, Call it what it is, a misunderstanding, doubt. Then offer the appropriate response to what is being raised, and check to see if your response has resolved the issue.

Again, your default personality settings come into play. People who are egocentric will tend to be more likely to ignore issues during a negotiation. Conversely, accommodators will tend to deal with the majority of issues raised in the process. This behavior is a classic manifestation of the tension between Relationship and Gain in a negotiation. If you're not happy with your negotiated results, then Stop Blaming the Fish.

Micro Strategies

So, now you have an insight into your defaults in dealings with others. You also have an understanding of what factors contribute to your location, where you are on the negotiating spectrum and the strengths and direction of your personality traits. It is time for you to take action. What are you going to do about it? Accept the consequences of your authentic self? Strive to become the next generation you? Or just live with the behaviors that are most destructive to your interactions? Gaining awareness and doing nothing is the easy way out. It takes no effort. If you continue to blame the fish at least you know that you are, in fact, rationalizing.

Here's your first step. Refer to the Negotiating Spectrum diagram on 31. Place an X along the continuum that represents your assessment of where you are today. Next place a circle with a dot in the middle of where you want to be on the continuum in a year. As established earlier, there are only two currencies in negotiations; Gain and Relationship. You are constantly trading perceived Relationship for perceived Gain and vice versa. It would seem like an easy enough task to keep these two in balance, but in practice, it's an incredibly difficult task. Why? Two import dynamics are affecting the balance; perception and context. The difficulty of managing the equity of Relationship and

Gain is that people have different perceptions of the value of what they represent and that Gain is much easier to quantify than its qualitative counterpart of Relationship. No magic formula or equation determines equity. Regrettably, they are subject to human interpretation.

The second dynamic is that perceived Gain and Relationship are contextually bound. That means the environment that you are in is in a permanent state of flux. Some environments are more stable than others and change at near glacial speed; others shift at the speed of the technology that supports them. A further complicating factor is that humans strive for permanence and stability. You fight most change. When you strike an agreement, you wish it to have permanence but that is not emblematic of the world you live. You fight to maintain gains even though the context is no longer in force. These factors are endemic to the human condition and must be addressed. The following pages outline two Micro Strategies: what to do if you default to **Relationship** and want to increase **Gain,** and what to do if you default to **Gain** and want to increase **Relationship.**

Recognize that these are not binary solutions, unless you are on the extreme of either Relationship or Gain. Craft your change intervention first to focus on those priority areas that are most detrimental to your ability to negotiate effectively, or you recognize you need to change. The first five tactics of both Micro Strategies are the same. This is because these tactics or practices are absolutely essential to achieving a successful negotiation no matter if your default is Relationship or Gain.

1. Ask, if the Juice is Worth the Squeeze

Before entering the field of combat, a skilled military leader always assesses the situation by asking these questions. Can I win? Is the battle worth it? Should I fight now, or would it be better to wait another day? What are the best, most likely and worst possible outcomes? Negotiators must also understand what's at stake, if you can win and, most importantly, if the negotiation battle is worthwhile.

Negotiations are not free. They consume resources, time and emotional energy. Sometimes submission may be the most expeditious, but also the most effective tactic. I love the opening quotation, "Is the juice worth the squeeze?" It is the quintessential question to determine if negotiating now, later or at all is appropriate. Measure the terrain, assess others, and determine what is to be gained or lost as you pick your battles. The intent is to avoid the 'lots of churn with no butter' syndrome.

2. Don't get into a Pissing Contest with a Skunk

You will always lose. So don't try! Skunks come in the form of con men, Social Darwinists and others who view negotiations as a sacred contest of wills. They live by the motto, "For me to win you have to lose." If you cannot change their game, then avoid the engagement, if at all possible. If you cannot avoid the engagement, proceed with extreme caution and employ all of the rules of power negotiations at your command.

3. Know What You Absolutely Need

Remember that a successful negotiation is one where all parties get what they need without irreparable damage to the relationship. Note that I said need, not want. Separating wants and needs is not only a semantic argument but also critical in negotiations. It is a subtlety that many do not grasp. This may be true not only for you, but the others with whom you negotiate as well. The fundamental but significant difference between a want and need is the number of possible solutions. Wants usually have one solution, whereas needs tend to have multiple options for solutions. For example, wanting a new BMW is markedly different than needing transportation to and from work. In the latter, a car is only one of multiple options that will satisfy the requirement for transportation. The options available include taking public transportation, walking, quitting your job, telecommuting or carpooling. They all can potentially satisfy that need versus buying a new BMW. Needs are driven by pain or opportunities not realized. They define a specific problem. Needs can be satisfied with multiple solution options, and these options create fallbacks. Wants do not, because they are solutions. The Rolling Stones' Mick Jagger and Keith Richards offer sage advice in the lyrics of their 1968 hit song, *You Can't Always Get What You Want*. The song counsels that you might not get what you want, but you should try to get what you need. That's a major difference in mindset; shifting from solution to problem focus. Take heed!

When you hear someone say they want something, always ask them what they need. It opens the door to a multitude of options that they might not have considered. Separating wants from needs is crucial to both problem resolving and negotiating. If you ask someone what he or she wants, it will usually only generate one specific option. Watch the words that you chose. Eliminate the word want and substitute need in its place. Practice by playing a mental game with yourself. Be aware and mindful of your word choices.

Remember that if the needs and wants are satisfied on both sides, there will be little compromise and the resolution may be durable. If only the needs of both parties are satisfied, the resolution may be practical, but may not endure. But if either party's needs are not satisfied, then the resolution is doomed to failure and usually backfires.

4. Know Your Defaults
By now you should have a good fix on your personality default settings. Are you social, limbic, accommodating, inquisitive and organized or are you reserved, calm, egocentric, non-curious and unstructured? These are two dipoles and there are many shades of gray between the two. The strength of the personality elements vary widely. Nonetheless, when pressure is applied you quickly tend to revert to our default settings. Know and be aware of how they manifest themselves when you negotiate. Are you too weak or over powering? If you're not happy with your negotiated results, then Stop Blaming the Fish.

5. Have a Fallback
One of the best ways to reduce pressure is to establish and create a fallback position, or a Plan B. Negotiations are all about how to handle situations. If you believe you have a situation that can only be resolved one way, you have no fallback. In other words, there are no other options and you abdicate any leverage you might have had in the situation.

Plan A is clearly your first choice. It's the one resolution to the situation that would work the best, but more often than not, a plan doesn't work out the way you had hoped. That's where Plan B, C, D and E come in. They give you options. They relieve the pressure you feel when you have to have to deal with a sole source. Remember always to establish at least one fallback. You don't have to use it; it just has to be there. Creating a fallback position may be more an illusion than reality. You should make others think that it is a viable alternative and you intend to use it if necessary. Having a fallback says that you have real options and you will decide on the best-balanced resolution. Think of these options as competition. If you are a buyer, whom will you choose to supply you? If you are a seller, whom will you choose to supply? Fallbacks may be other competitors, make versus buy or a new disruptive technology.

There are fallbacks other than having to buy or sell. One fallback that you always have is choosing not to agree, a deferral, an intermittent 'deadlock' or pause in the action. This pause in the negotiation serves as an excellent fallback--it can restore your sense of power and may keep you from sweating it out. In a negotiation, the only place that you have to be real is in the mind of others. Flexibility will always increase leverage in a negotiation. It is derived from clearly separating your needs from your wants. The ability to separate the two is something most people get very confused about.

The ultimate fallback position can be litigation, particularly in a litigious society like the United States. You might say that going to litigation is extreme, which is true, but if you have no other options, it may be your only fallback. Use the legal route discretely, because it is extremely expensive and time-consuming. Someone always wins, and someone always loses. There are some who believe that entering the legal realm is a lose-lose proposition, but again the threat of uncertainty of winning may drive the win-win. How many times have people gone to court initially then settled the matter out of court? The vast majority of the legal system would overload and grind to a halt without these out-of-court settlements.

If you default to Relationship and want to move toward Gain, then continue reading the following seven tactics (6-12). If you default to Gain and want to move toward Relationship, then skip to page 58.

6. Assess Your Leverage

It is always better to work from a position of strength. You have more power than you think you do. You tend to focus on your shortcomings and amplify the strengths of others. It is a natural human phenomenon, part of our human condition. The secret to overcoming this problem is to do a reality check. Get the emotion, the baggage, the negative self-talk and ego out of the process. Stick to the facts and assess the relative power balance in a negotiation. I offer one caveat about this activity; be prepared to reassess. Negotiation is a process of discovery. You rarely have perfect knowledge and, if you are receptive, you learn more as you journey through the process. You have more leverage in a negotiation than you think.

7. Leave Room

Always ask for more than what you are willing to take. Leave yourself room to negotiate. Building in negotiating room gives you the latitude to maneuver. It allows others to realize their expectations and feel as if they have also won. It provides space so that you can test and determine reality. Approach the idea of asking for more by examining where the big mistakes are made in negotiating.

Another reason to ask for more is that people discount your requests. If I asked someone to change their opinion about a topic, most would adjust their opinion somewhat, but rarely accept the entire shift. Researchers say that the greater the request for a shift, the more willingly people accept change. This holds true until the demand is viewed as outrageous, manipulative or ridiculous. Once that point is reached, then credibility is out the window. So again, set your sights on being near but not exceeding the absurd or the ridiculous. The trick is that you're dealing with people, and people have differing views of where that point resides. Spend time anticipating where the point of the absurdity in an opening offer might be for the person with whom you will be negotiating.

Where do people screw up in a negotiation? There is no one place or one reason, but in my experience, I have observed four extremely sensitive times where mistakes often occur. They happen when you are setting your expectations for the outcome of a negotiation, making initial offers to buy or sell, making mistakes, or saying something without thinking and are engaged in pressure bargaining.

8. Set High Expectations, but Don't Trust Them

Our perceptions largely drive our expectations. Expectations are highly susceptible to the Rosenthal Effect--they tend to become a self-fulfilling prophecy. Our perceptions are a combination of facts, beliefs, biases, intuition, experiences, and gut feelings. Expectation setting in a negotiation should not be approached in a cavalier, fly-by-the-seat-of-your-pants way. All trained aviators know that flying-by-the-seat-of-your-pants can be both deceiving and dangerous. It's deceiving in that your senses create the wrong perception of what is happening and send erroneous information to your brain causing inappropriate and unsafe behavior. Aviators, who experience vertigo, have flown perfectly airworthy planes into the ground. They get into a death spiral and are unable to recover because they wrongly perceive their environment. In negotiations, these practices can cause a misdiagnosis of what is occurring:

- Determine what your expectations are. What are the best, worst and most likely outcomes, and why? Plan your fallback position.
- Project what you think the expectations of the other party might be. What are the best, worst and most likely outcomes for them, and why do you think that's the case? What do you anticipate their fallback to be?
- Plan the questions you will ask as a test to confirm or refute these assumed expectations.

Be painfully aware that your initial offer defines the top or bottom of the negotiating space. Be deliberate and leave room to negotiate. Why? Because most rational people expect a degree of give and take in the dance that is negotiating. Also, you do not know where the other party's expectations reside. Be prepared to give a rationale for your opening offers and legitimize the offer with evidence whenever possible. Make others work to get a concession from the opener. Never make a gratuitous concession; it confuses people.

The consequences of having an opening offer that leaves you room to negotiate but exceeds the other party's expectations of the desired outcome can be devastating to you in the results of a negotiation. Be careful; like first impressions, you only get one chance to make an opening offer. If it's wrong, you are propelled into damage control mode.

9. Determine the Other's Game
Behaviors, not words, determine intent and point to your opponent's negotiating style, strategy, and tactics. You cannot play win-win with someone who is playing win-lose with you unless you force a lose-lose. That may cause a change in their strategy.

When you negotiate, the pie is sometimes limited, and the negotiation becomes about how to divide it. This action defines the realm of positional or distributive negotiation. Win-win resolutions can occur even if there is a fixed pie, but both parties must exhibit a willingness to collaborate. Negotiators can enter the positional arena that is driven by a win-lose mentality without true collaboration. One way to ensure that the pie will be divided equitably is to have one of the parties cut it and allow the other party to choose the piece that they want. It is critically important to avoid applying the rules of positional negotiation to all negotiating situations. The problem with the positional approach is that it doesn't relate well to the dynamics of today's environment. Few negotiations in today's business environment are once and done. The negotiators must always remember that nothing is permanent, power tends to shift and there will always be a tomorrow.

Positional negotiations are characterized as being short term in focus and competitive in nature. It's driven by a win-lose mentality characterized by the buyer wanting to buy at the lowest possible price and the seller wanting to sell at the highest price. Negotiations conducted in this arena usually wind up in a zero sum game. That is, if I get more pie that means you will get less. Contrast that to negotiations where the party's intent is to create mutual gain by capitalizing on synergies. They tend to be characterized by a more cooperative approach, where increasing the mutual gain is the strategy. Expanding the pie and sharing the incremental value creates a win-win result.

It is important to understand that win-win like win-lose is not a result, but a mindset. It's a way of seeing the world, a lens to view situations. Neither mindset is wrong nor right, they just are. The reality is that to be effective today, you must be able to play win-win, win-lose and every other game on the continuum. The choice of the game you play is not an either or, but all of the above. You must be able to interpret the game of others and respond accordingly.

10. Get Others to Move First, Set Deadlines and Ask for Commitments

All positional negotiations must involve a degree of give and take, but the question is how much is each party willing to move? That is achieved during the process of discovery in positional negotiations. A skilled negotiator always assesses the situation and anticipates what they believe to be the negotiating space, but the assessment is usually based on assumptions of the other person's position, strengths, vulnerabilities, expectations, and urgencies. That's why the first offer, which is usually some concession, is so critically important. It is usually driven by a combination of our expectations and what you believe are the other person's expectations.

This first round of give and take is wrought with risk. Your actions are being driven by assumptions, estimates, and conjecture. So the safe bet is to get others to make the first offer. How do you determine if an offer or concession is meaningful? What does meaningful mean? Who determines what's meaningful? By making a low-ball opening offer, can you encourage others? Let's look at these questions one by one, but first let's be clear that the expectations of others drives what is meaningful, not our expectations.

How do you determine what might be meaningful? As stated earlier, in the early stages of a negotiation you have lots of untested assumptions, estimates, and conjecture. The more you plan and anticipate, the more precise our intelligence of others will be. The best way to determine what's meaningful to others is to have them tell us, without realizing what they are giving away. This might be accomplished through skillful questioning cast in a problem-resolving context, not a negotiating context. Trust and rapport are crucial if you want to get honest information from others. If these elements are not present, the best strategy is to go slowly and talk around, but never make a concession. At this phase of the negotiation, what you might consider a concession that has little value might have the opposite effect on others. Never, ever make a gratuitous concession. Make people work to receive any concession. If you don't make them work, it will encourage them to ask for more

What does meaningful really mean, and who determines it? Meaningful is what resides in the expectations and the needs of others. Their assessment, needs, desires, and perceptions of value create meaning. If a concession signals that their expectation will be reached, then you have made a meaningful concession in the mind of others. This perceived concession could be true even if it was a low-ball opening offer. Your concession might have encouraged others if their expectations were low. A meaningful concession signals to others that their expectations are going to be met and that there may be more to gain. That's the dangerous part. Once expectations are met or exceeded, few people recalibrate new expectations. Most people go for more, pushing to see how much more they can get. The irony of the situation is that it was our meaningful concession that triggered a change in the expectations of others. It may not be a new concrete expectation, but it is now certainly higher than before.

Unilateral concessions are a bad strategy. Strive to make any concession conditional. That is, put a string on the concession, so if it is not accepted, you can pull it back, like a yo-yo. Unilateral concessions are gratuitous in that they are given without consequence. Concessions with strings can take the form of time-bound offers, reciprocal concessions or contractual commitments. When asked to make a concession, always ask for equitable consideration in return. Since the offer is conditional, if it's not accepted, it's off the table.

The longer a negotiation drags out, the more information winds up in the public forum, equaling the leverage. One critically important note here is that you should always establish a deadline in your negotiations. Deadlines can always be renegotiated, but if there is no deadline, a great incentive to reach a conclusion or close is absent. Without a deadline, nothing happens.

Along with establishing a deadline, always ask when is the right time to negotiate. When will I have the greatest leverage? Something that usually comes into play in a negotiation is referred to as the regret principle. It states that the value of what is received is always higher before it has been delivered. Practically speaking, you are generally in a better space to negotiate before you commit rather than after. Buyer's remorse is another artifact of the same sentiment.

11. Ask, Don't Tell and Shut Up

Sales people tend to think that their job is to convince and persuade by talking. Most sales professionals have been traditionally selected because of good social skills and an outgoing personality. But when you are talking, persuading, convincing or influencing you are not listening. When you are talking, you are giving information, not getting it. When in doubt, shut up!

This problem is exacerbated by the fact that you tend to think that selling and negotiating are separate and discrete activities. Most sales processes have several phases to them. One of those phases is usually called negotiating or hard bargaining. It is as if you miraculously transition from selling to negotiating when in reality it just doesn't happen that way. Again, selling determines if you are going to do business, and negotiating determines how the business will be done. They happen simultaneously and are inextricably connected.

Most communications experts state that truly meaningful dialogue requires the conversation to be balanced. Most negotiations are not intended to engage in meaningful dialogue. These negotiations are about give and take, or trade-offs. If you are giving, others are taking. The negotiator must be able to discern and validate the strategy of others and act accordingly. If the game is positional, then you're playing win-lose. Create a vacuum of silence and be comfortable with it. Silence is a practice, and it will pay dividends quickly.

It has been said that it is far better to be interested than interesting. Most of us gravitate toward interesting. How does someone become interesting, by being charming, charismatic, dynamic and entertaining? All of these descriptors share at least these common attributes: being persuasive and selling yourself. Salespeople think of themselves as people-people. They are usually likable, have good personalities and can carry a conversation. These attributes predispose them to talk a lot, giving away potentially critical information and intelligence. Be very careful.

12. Don't Be Gratuitous

What is trust? At its core, trust is having confidence that someone will behave as you expect. It's not judging good or bad behavior, but predictable behavior. It is a subjective process at best, and for many of us deciding to trust someone is based on our beliefs about the true nature of humanity. Who you trust comes from the answer to this question, is man good or evil by nature? Of course, no one knows the answer to the question, and it cannot be proven either way, but many people go through life believing that man's basic nature is one way, which drives how they view others and subsequently how they grant trust. Remember that most promises are not kept.

Trust is the predictability that someone will deliver on a commitment or behave as anticipated during a negotiation. It is not a measure of goodness or virtue, but simply whether events will unfold as expected. Predictability is prone to error. There is always a risk in trying to predict if you need to add goodness into the equation when determining if you should trust someone.

It is naïve to pretend that everything and everyone is good and wonderful. Do not expect or assume good intent from others. The logical negotiating approach is to suspect everything and everyone until proven trustworthy, particularly when you have had limited experience with others. If you gratuitously trust people, then you are inviting disaster. Make them earn it. Remember, in desperate times, people do desperate things. So, how does one determine if someone is trustworthy or not? It is determined by watching the behaviors of other people.

In addition to not trusting gratuitously a corollary behavior is not to concede gratuitously. Concessions take many forms from dropping price, adding services, accepting information provided as fact, extending deadlines to not securing hard commitments. All of these have currency in negotiations. Don't simply give them away. Make people earn what they get. Learn to put strings on concessions that you make. "I'll do that in return for this." Hold people accountable for missing deadlines. Test information they provide by asking good questions. Most people perceive that if they receive a gratuitous concession it has little value. The converse may be true, but since the concession wasn't earned, but given, it is discounted.

If you default to Gain and want to move toward Relationship, then your Micro Strategy includes these additional tactics (if you default to Relationship you already completed your tactics and can skip to Chapter 5):

6. Share the Air Time

Airtime is the amount of time that you are talking or dominating a meeting. Although there is no magic number, less is more in most meetings. Sharing the airtime has several simultaneous benefits; it allows others to engage, it builds a more collaborative environment, it legitimizes other points of view, and it allows for discovery. A word of caution, if you have identified yourself as Social or an extrovert your propensity is to talk. That chews up airtime at the exclusion of others. When a thought is triggered, many people interrupt others so they don't forget the thought. If this is you, make a note and interject at the appropriate time. Sharing airtime takes conscious effort and is not easy to master.

7. Move from a Solution to a Problem Focus

You live in a solution-focused culture, not one that appreciates problems. Ergo, solutions are good, and problems are bad. People aren't usually rewarded for unearthing problems, but they are rewarded for creating solutions. The quicker you can come up with a solution the more you are rewarded. Are advertisements trying to sell problems? No, they are offering solutions.

This cultural dynamic of solution focus is pervasive in negotiations and is counter productive. Solution focus is particularly evident in positional negotiations where all parties have expectations of reaching a pre-defined solution. Solution focus does have its place, but it should follow a clear and shared understanding of the problem. Leaders need to create a vision where there is none. John F. Kennedy's goal of putting a man on the moon by the end of the 1960's was, in fact, a national unifying solution. Having grown up in that era, I don't remember anyone asking, "what's the problem that putting a man on the moon going to solve?" More often than not, visions that are solutions are half-baked, have little support because stakeholders are confused about the intent, lack granularity and details, are incredibly hard to execute and have a limited shelf life depending on the context within which they were created. Even leadership solutions fall prey to the maxim that there is a fine line between vision and hallucination.

Once defined, the problem needs to be categorized. In reality, not everything is negotiable. There is, in fact, a limited array of problem types that you can resolve using the negotiating process. Negotiation can resolve disputes that encompass a host of business and personal issues including the value of goods and services that are not fixed, claims, terms and conditions of doing business, liability, confidentiality, ownership of intellectual property and other issues. You can also negotiate remedies for problems with an uncertainty of future conditions and breach. In some cases you can apply negotiations to a dilemma, agreeing on the lesser of bad options. Additional problem types that are not amenable to resolution by negotiation are those with a known and accepted correct answer, morale or political impasse, problems with a multitude of variables and options, and those requiring a clear vision or goal.

As a starting point, focus on securing an agreement to determine what is the shared goal; what is wrong, what is not working or what needs to be changed. Doing so increases the likelihood of reaching a workable and durable resolution.

8. Honor Commitments

Getting and honoring commitments are flip sides of the same coin. Getting commitments deals with avoiding unilateral commitments, which is a prescription for disaster. In securing a commitment from another, it must be specific and time bound. 'I'll get back to you soon' is not a commitment and shows no loyalty to resolving an issue. Be careful how you get commitments from others. Demands are counter-productive if you are trying to improve relationships.

The rule for honoring commitments is simple. Do what you commit to and don't commit if you cannot or don't intend on delivering.

9. Stay Focused

The single most important ability a negotiator must possess is the ability to stay calm and focused under fire. Don't let them see you sweat. Once you enter the realm of emotion, things usually get out of control quickly. Emotions severely impact your ability to think rationally and respond. Consequently, your ability to negotiate may be compromised. In addition to dealing with the present set of circumstances, you are loading your mind with past baggage and the negative consequences of the future. You outstrip your mind's ability to think clearly and focus. Your physical being will be the first indicator that this phenomenon is occurring. If you feel yourself getting flushed, your mind racing, your pulse increasing, or feel unable to focus and think, then call a time out.

In sport, when one team has lost their edge and another team has gained an advantage, you can see and feel it. That's when the other team calls a time out to regroup. In negotiations, just as in a sport, a time out is called to re-center and regain focus on the moment. Its aim is to disregard thoughts about the two dimensions of time that you cannot control, the past and future, and concentrate on the now. The present is the only dimension of time that you can control. You make decisions in the now that become your past and shape your future, but they are made in the present, so stay in the here and now.

The past and the future are usually used in negotiating to evoke responses from the other party. They are intended to shift leverage. When dealing with this issue, a mantra that I have used to re-center myself is, "honor the past, acknowledge the present, and create the future." It's a perspective-adjusting device. The past *is*. There is nothing that you can do to change what has already happened. So, honor the past as it is, and move on. Judging the past is an exercise in futility because you do it with 20/20 hindsight corrected through the lens of our point of view. The decisions of the past were made under different circumstances, using different filters and lenses that probably have changed. In short, the past is done. Move on.

The decisions and actions you take at this moment impact the future. When Julius Caesar crossed the Rubicon, when John F. Kennedy set a goal to land a man on the moon by the end of the 1960's, when Hitler invaded Poland, these acts at the moment set in motion a chain of events that created a future. Newtonian Law talks about equal and opposite reactions. This law is predictable in nature, but regrettably not so in humans. The human reaction, albeit somewhat predictable according to personality type, can elicit an array of responses to a particular situation. In any case, staying in the moment and being cool and focused will always provide a better environment for making decisions.

10. Be Civil

What does it mean to demonstrate civility? Civility is defined as courtesy and politeness, and recognizing humanity, worth, and dignity. Too often, power plays attempt to do the opposite. Respecting a person's presence is an elegant act; the small investment of time it takes to acknowledge another person pays back many times. Just remembering a person's name, something about what was going on in their lives the last time you met, a head nod in their direction, or even just direct eye contact (if it is culturally acceptable), can work wonders.

If negotiating outside of your country of origin, understanding and complying with culture norms and customs are critical to the process of effectively acknowledging others. As an account manager with a Fortune 250 company, I was required to make joint visits with senior management to important accounts. One of these accounts was in Toronto, Canada. During a meeting with the senior management of this critical account, my Vice President and

General Manager started his presentation by saying that he appreciated being invited to Toronto, the most cosmopolitan city in the United States. Wow, that was a hard act to follow. It does illustrate that Americans tend to extrapolate our borders, norms, values and behaviors to the rest of the world. In this case, ignorance turned a gesture that was meant to be an acknowledgment of the cosmopolitan city of Toronto into an insult. Innocent, you may say, but the gesture backfired. Instead of building rapport or a relationship, it perpetuated an American stereotype. If you negotiate internationally, be sure you are aware of local customs and observe them to the highest degree possible. The consequences of not observing local customs will undermine your real intent to acknowledge others.

Be inclusive: invite others to the negotiating table as co-problem definers and co-problem resolvers. Being inclusive means acceptance of the other person's value. It means not dominating the conversation and not having to make your position known. Share control and invite others to express their views and ideas without being judgmental.

Be kind: There are hundreds of clichés about how kindness works and aggressiveness or nastiness doesn't. Kindness is not soft. On the contrary, speaking kindly sets you up for success.

What does it mean to speak kindly? There is more to speaking kindly than just omitting any trash talking, use of foul language, offensive jokes or comments, loud and boisterous speech, and an over abundance of hubris. This reminds me of the time when a woman moved next door to me. Our first meeting was cordial and pleasant. The second meeting was impromptu at the local market. After an exchange of niceties, she related a story from her old neighborhood about an Italian family "Guineaing" up the neighborhood with garish landscaping. Being ethnically Italian, I was offended by her thoughtless use of a racial slur describing Italian-Americans. Kindness in discussion stems from more than just restricting yourself to polite tone and dialogue; you must consider the content of your words.

Be respectful: Respect and acknowledgment of the opinions of others are not agreement. To acknowledge someone's opinion only means that you understand that they may have a difference of views, and you respect their right to have one. It validates their humanity and intellect. Too often, people feel that they must defeat another person's opinion by proving them wrong and winning the argument. This behavior does little to find a middle or common ground and create a mutual reality.

Be mindful of space: Space can be violated when someone penetrates your personal buffer zone, gives you an unwelcome touch and offers a kiss as a greeting when one is not warranted or expected. These are all violations of personal space, the boundaries of which have no universal definition. It is personal, and not absolute. For clues on proper encroachment, be sensitive and conscious of people's reaction to you as you approach them. To be safe, whatever distance you historically allowed as a buffer, add 50 percent more space to it.

During a visit with my 93-year-old Italian mother, I learned that she doesn't like being kissed on the lips. She prefers the European air-kiss on the cheek method. Why? Germs. I assumed that this was a new phobia, so I asked. Her response was that she had never liked kissing on the lips and was repulsed by people casually kissing her on the lips. I was taken aback, not because of what she said, but because all of the time I have known her I had been blind to her need for germ-free, personal space.

Be mindful of time: Being fashionably late doesn't mean failing to show up at all. Honoring commitment of time speaks volumes about a person's respect for another person. It is indicative of how you behave in other situations. If you cannot be trusted to be here when you said you would arrive, how can you be trusted with other more substantial commitments? "I'm always late" is not an acceptable excuse. If you know you are not going to be able to make a commitment, then don't commit to it. Tardiness is particularly frustrating to someone who is fastidiously punctual

Some of us go through life rarely challenging what you have come to believe as truth. For others, experience, education or a significant emotional event can trigger a wholesale reevaluation of what you believe and hold dear. Regardless, whether or not belief systems are evolved, they exist and form the basis of one's reality. They need to be respected and acknowledged. After all, when does something become a myth? Only after you stop believing it to be true.

11. Stay on the Same Page

If the result of a negotiation requires durability and equity, then do not advance to the next step in the process until all stakeholders in a negotiation are in the same place at the same time. By process, I mean whatever process you are attempting to complete; answering an objection, defining terms, developing a problem statement, understanding expectations, dealing with emotions, etc. If one party is ahead or behind, that will create confusion and possible miscommunication that can impact trust. To avoid getting disconnected and to stay on the same page follow these key actions:

Develop, Syndicate and Agree on an Agenda. In my experience, this relatively simple action is not done as a routine practice for negotiations or meetings. The agenda is a roadmap for the discussions that are to take place. It starts the process of making significant agreements one little agreement at a time. Taking the initiative to draft the agenda gives you the opportunity to shape the conversation. Syndicating provides others with an opportunity to add their input while agreement means that it is common and shared.

Make certain that you are understood and that you understand. Words are names you use to describe things and concepts. By their nature, they are not exact, although lawyers claim that they are. Without definitions, sadly, there would be no place for lawyers. I maintain that many in the legal profession tend to exploit this ambiguity and make things more complex and subject to interpretation solely to promote its ends. If agreements are not precise, then they are subject to interpretation and legal opinion. And you all have opinions. When I utter a word or group of words, it creates some mental image in your head. If you are communicating effectively, then your understanding of the concept or idea I shared matches what I intended to share with you, and visa versa. All too often, you assume that people understand what you are saying as you intended. If you layer on the connotations of words, people's interpretation and history associated with them, it is a wonder that anyone understands what anyone else is trying to say.

I was once a supervisor for a group of sales people at a time when the company raised prices resulting in many upset customers who began looking for other alternatives. Many even stopped buying from the company. The business situation turned rather bleak, so I decided to charge up my team with a pep talk saying you aren't going to walk away from any more business. A simple, straightforward message, wouldn't you agree?

Let's look at how each of the team members interpreted "You aren't going to walk away from any more business." One took my comment to mean that if a competitive situation arises in the future, you'll meet it. Another thought I meant they should go back to every customer who stopped buying from us and slash prices to regain their business. Still, another thought I said that you needed to sell harder and deemphasize pricing discussions. One statement resulted in three interpretations. Who's right and who's wrong?

No one was correct, and all of us were at fault. I should have clarified what I meant by that short statement. My team should have challenged me to be more specific. Why didn't that happen? Conventional wisdom would say that the team should have just used their just common sense. Common sense leads to three different conclusions. Common sense was not the problem, common behavior was. What I wanted, but failed to articulate, was a common practice of not losing any more business based upon price. I should have been clearer, and they should have asked for clarity.

Everyone wants to appear smart and knowledgeable, sometimes at the expense of complete understanding. Unless you're clairvoyant or a super intellect, most of us don't get it the first time. There's no shame in asking for clarification.

Get the consent of others before proceeding to the next step. Since you are dealing with a problem resolving process, it is critical to reach closure and agreement on one issue or process before moving to the next. Permission to move on is the essence of staying on the same page. It is incumbent on all parties to address concerns during each step of the negotiating process before advancing to the next step. Too often, negotiators attempt to drive their point of view without sufficient consideration and idea gestation time. Not allowing this time sets up a win-lose dynamic, which may lead to distrust. If others in the negotiation perceive that you are attempting to persuade, manipulate or intimidate them to accept your point of view, you risk leaving the more balanced and productive problem resolving space and entering the world of horse-trading. At this point, people tend to become suspicious, guarded and much less cooperative. Agreements should be made one small agreement at a time, not in a big bang fashion.

It is critical that you temper our predisposition to jump to a solution before fully defining and understanding the problem.

Manage Disagreements Productively. During any phase of the resolution process, objections, or differences of thought, will surface. As in all problem-resolving interactions, you always have three response options. You can ignore the objection, defer it to be addressed later, or deal with it. It has been my experience that when objections are raised you usually have to deal with it or face becoming disconnected. A great technique to assess if the issue is real or not is to ask others: "Are you serious?" Be careful to use a non-threatening tone of voice and non-verbal gestures. Surprisingly, if the objection is gratuitous, they will back off quickly. Ignoring is another way of testing to see if the objection is real. You must be masterful at this technique, because it can easily backfire if poorly executed.

For example, our current home had hardwood floors and required the purchase of many area rugs when we first moved in. There are many other rug dealers in our area, but Joe the Rag Merchant was extremely knowledgeable about rugs. He provided excellent guidance on value and what to buy based upon intended use. He was also a great storyteller, who painted a picture of a rug being made in some exotic land by skilled craftsmen one knot at a time, blending the exquisitely dyed skills and wools into a one-of-a-kind masterpiece. Some of our selections were expensive hand knotted rugs, and others were the more reasonably priced synthetic, machine-made variety. When it came time to negotiate, Joe ignored any overtures to discuss price. He simply continued to write up an invoice with the price marked on the tag and took the conversation in an entirely different direction. He pivoted. He talked about his new grandchild, the youth development program that he hosts on the upper level of his store, and anything else but price. His technique caused me to forget that I raised the price issue at all. In retrospect, Joe practiced all of the skills and techniques that we have discussed. Unless you are Joe, who has his craft mastered, be very careful of ignoring objections.

12. Engage to Persuade

The theory doesn't *always* work, the point is that the more you get people involved in the decision, the more ownership they have and the easier it is to close on an agreement. Some problem resolving tools to help with the process of engaging to persuade are:

Objectify and Depersonalize the Issue. Never make the person into the problem. Objectify and depersonalize it by making the problem separate from the person attempting to resolve it. This technique allows the parties to work collaboratively on it, rather than point fingers, make accusations or deal with the emotional baggage.

Agree on the Problem. After making the problem an "it," give it a name to which all parties can agree. A problem is a multi-dimensional object. As you turn the object, you get a different perspective or view. One party's view is two dimensional and limited. The totality of the picture lies in the collective view. Remember that perception by definition is a reality, however, that reality may not be accurate.

Once the problem is defined, then ownership of the problem can be discussed.

By encouraging a genuine, collaborative discussion on defining the problem, a complete view of the problem is developed, and a face-saving exit is opened for those who had an inaccurate perception of the problem.

Play with Ideas: Encourage Exploration of Needs, Options, and Consequences. I like to start with a straw model or rough draft of a problem statement to kick-start the process, be careful not to try to use it to manipulate the situation or persuade others. It is imperative that a spirit of openness to modifying the straw model be sincere. If it is not, credibility and trust may be lost for the duration of the negotiation.

Persuasion will result from effectively involving people, not dazzling them with your brilliance or baffling them with inaccuracies, lies, and misrepresentations. People tend to believe more in what they say themselves than what others may tell them. A sense of choice and progress tends to motivate most people to engage in problem resolution dialogue.

Advances in learning technology for both children and adults point out that play can be catalytic in helping people understand concepts, retain knowledge and foster buy-in. So when you throw an idea into the discussion, and someone picks it up and starts playing with it and changing it to fit their thought process, you have a choice. You can either become upset that someone is co-opting your great idea and not recognizing your brilliance and insightfulness, or you can relish the fact that someone else thinks your idea is good and is playing with it to make it their own. The essence of persuading involves others in the process. A classic example is a customer liking the way they look in the suit that you asked them to try on.

There is an element of selflessness required in persuading someone. We all appreciate being recognized to varying degrees. When another takes the idea that you have planted and runs with it, you may lose ownership and credit for it, but if you were attempting to persuade you have succeeded. When people play with your ideas, they will tend to change them. Be careful not to get upset at losing control of your creation. Remember, the objective is to make your idea their idea.

Persuasion is a continuum. It ranges from Apathy to Commitment. It defines the level of alignment with others and the behavioral cues indicative of that state. If you pay attention, others will emote concrete indicators of the issues that are preventing them from commitment. In fact, most people will not be immediately or wholly persuaded to buy what you're selling, they usually will challenge your idea or suggestion. They're neither accepting nor rejecting it; they are testing its efficacy. Opposition, provided you can discover further what is at the root of what they are opposing, can be positive. People may oppose what you say for one of four reasons; they have a misunderstanding of your statement, they don't believe what you are purporting, there is something incorrect or flawed in what you said, or they perceive a drawback to what was offered. Once you can define and validate the basis of their opposition, you can address the issue straight away. Don't view opposition as a negative situation, but an opportunity to advance the process of persuasion if you can successfully deal with their objections.

Consider the Problem in Context. Context provides meaning to facts. Most facts that are taken out of context can be manipulated into half-truths. Facts are the currency of arguments. Arguments are used in debate to make a case. They rely primarily on one type of approach; you are either for or against alternatives. The more facile and convincing a presenter is in manipulating facts, the more successful he or she will be in persuading others. The purpose of this section is defensive in nature; simply remember to consider the context when facts are presented to you.

Facts offer proof or give validity to an argument. Proof or evidence can also come in several forms with varying levels of confidence associated with the form. The least credible and lowest form of evidence is anecdotal. It is episodic, non-statistically based, but irrefutable. The efficacy of evidence can be determined by the protocol, rigor, and breath of the event that produced the resultant conclusion. Always ask: "What is different about the context of the proof now versus when it was generated?" Evidence can always be manipulated to suit the position of others. It is the context that can provide a reality check on the validity and sustainability of the fact. Facts are only true in the context in which they were discovered. If the circumstances surrounding the fact remain constant, consider it a fact. However, if the context appreciably changes from the time of discovery to the time the fact is called into an argument, consider the fact suspect. This practice will ensure that both parties stay on the same page.

At this point you have now identified where you are on the Negotiating Spectrum. You should have a clear picture of your hard-wired settings, whether you favor Relationship or Gain, whether you are Limbic or Calm, prefer organized or unstructured environments, are reserved or social, and whether you are intellectually curious or not. You have identified the direction you need to move to be a better-balanced negotiator and created a plan to manage your change. Now it's up to you. If you're usually not happy with your negotiated results, it's time to take control and Stop Blaming the Fish.

Chapter V - Docking The Boat

"The most dangerous creation of any society is the man who has nothing to lose."

James Baldwin

I leave you with a crucial parting warning and a challenge. Perhaps this is the greatest negotiating lesson to be learned. Regrettably our world is rich with examples of the realization of Baldwin's quote. It is a grim foreshadowing. Remember those words. Apply them to your day-to-day negotiations and never push too far. Your perception by definition is your reality, but it may not be accurate. Whenever someone feels rightly or wrongly like they have lost, in their mind they have lost. Your winning today may result in your losing tomorrow.

When we learn a new way or method, we tend to run ourselves into the ground experimenting with it. Like dieting or starting an exercise regime, we tend to overreact at times, burn ourselves out and then resort to our old habits. If you attempt to change your behavior to shift the Gain/Relationship balance, it will come at a price and requires commitment. When you try to change any behavior it takes work and creates stress. Practicing new behaviors feels uncomfortable and unnatural. Our responses are no longer automatic. Behavioral change takes conscious effort and increased awareness. Everything in life comes at a price. To leave your comfort zone you must commit to consciously changing YOU. Remember the fable at the beginning? Sometimes you may attempt to conjure lame excuses, blinded by your self-interests by blaming others or making excuses for problems created by your own doing. If you're not happy with your current negotiated results, then Stop Blaming the Fish.

Chapter VI - The Tackle Box

"It is not from the benevolence of the butcher, the brewer, or the baker that we expect our dinner, but from their regard to their interest."

Adam Smith

Like the fisherman's tackle box this section contains rich definitions of terms used to describe the Negotiating Spectrum and Personality Trait Maps that will serve as a resource to hone your skill as a better-balanced negotiator.

DEFINITIONS & EXPLANATIONS FOR THE NEGOTIATING SPECTRUM:

Negotiating Style:	Selfless Givers	Strategic Givers	Matchers	Takers	Social Darwinists
Strategy:	Avoid Conflict	Pay-it-forward	Quid pro quo	Defeat	Crush
Tactics:	Appease	Accede Collaborate Compromise	Collaborate Persuade Influence Compromise Bargain Power Play Coerce	Bargain Power Play Coerce	Power Play Coerce
Default:	Relationship				Gain
Adaptability:	Accommodat				Egocentric
Empathy:	Too Much				None
Propensity to Find Opportunities to Negotiate	Avoid				Find
Perspective on Availabilty of Resources	Plenty				Scarcity

Negotiating Spectrum

Strategies

Given our natural negotiating style coupled with the perceptions of a situation seen through the lens of our location filters, you create a strategy to accomplish an outcome. Each of the strategies can have multiple tactical approaches in its arsenal. Remember, strategy determines what you want or desire to do, not how you will do it. Tactics are the operationalization of strategy. They are specific, actionable and more granular.

Avoid Conflict

Conflict avoidance is a method of dealing with conflict by directly avoiding confronting the issue at hand. Methods of doing this can include changing the subject, putting off a discussion until later (and not bringing up the subject of contention), giving in to others, appeasement or acquiescing. Conflict avoidance can be used as a temporary measure to buy time or as permanent means of disposing of the matter. The latter may be indistinguishable from simple acquiescence, to the extent that the person avoiding the conflict subordinates their wishes to others with which there is a potential conflict. However, conflict avoidance can also take the form of withdrawing from the relationship. Thus, avoidance scenarios tend to result in win-lose or lose-lose, if terminating the relationship is the best method of solving the problem.

Pay-it-forward

Pay-it-forward is a personal strategy to fulfill one's need for social responsibility. It is an <u>ethical</u> framework and suggests that an individual has an obligation to act for the benefit of society as a whole. Social responsibility is a duty every individual has to perform so as to maintain a balance between the economy and the ecosystems. A trade-off may exist between economic development, in the material sense, and the welfare of the society and environment. Social responsibility means the equilibrium between the two. It pertains not only to business organizations but also to individual actions. This responsibility can be passive, by avoiding engaging in socially harmful acts, or active, by performing activities that directly advance social goals.

Pay-it-forward employs the concept of reciprocal altruism. The idea suggests that altruism is the act of helping someone else while incurring some cost with the understanding that there is the possibility of payback (i.e. being in a reverse situation where the individual who was helped before may perform an altruistic act towards the person who helped them).

Quid Pro Quo
Quid pro quo from the Latin means something for something. Another way of expressing this expectation is tit for tat, which is based an English saying from 1556; "tip for tap," which literally means, blow for blow, or retaliation in kind. Retaliation is also known as payback, retribution, revenge or vengeance; it may be characterized as a form of justice or more broadly, an equivalent to an action given in return. It has related meanings and used as a concept in business, as well as in the mathematical area of game theory. The concept is exemplified in real world negotiations in the form of reciprocated concessions and compromise for managing activities to reach an agreement or resolve a dispute.

Defeat
In this context, the definition of the expectation of defeat uses the verb form of the word; that is to win a victory over (someone) in a battle or other contest; to overcome or beat. Winning by any means possible and at any cost is the operative intent. Winning may also be interpreted as losing less than the other.

Crush
The expectation of Crush is an order of magnitude greater than Defeat. Words that describe or exemplify this strategy are to suppress, put down, quash, stamp out, end, overpower, break, repress, subdue, extinguish, or annihilate. The intent of the engagement or exchange is not merely to win, but to utterly destroy without empathy.

Examples of this expectation are plentiful in the neo-Machiavellian work, *The 48 Laws of Power* by Robert Greene. The laws offered in this book go well beyond the competitive rules of negotiating. Law 15 best exemplifies the book's sentiment and expectation, "Crush your enemy totally --- All great leaders since Moses have known that a feared enemy must be crushed completely. (Sometimes they have learned this the hard way.) If one ember is left alight, no matter how dimly it smolders, a fire will eventually break out. More is lost through stopping halfway than through total annihilation: The enemy will recover, and will seek revenge. Crush him, not only in body but spirit."

Tactics
A tactic is an action or collection of actions that are crafted and planned to achieve a particular end. They can include a: scheme, plan, maneuver, method, expedient, gambit, move, approach, tack, device, trick, ploy, dodge, ruse, machination, contrivance, policy and a campaign. It is manifested in action, not intent.

Appease
The process of appeasement is defined by conciliation, placation, concession, pacification and propitiation. The hallmark of appeasement in this context is unilateral concession making to avoid conflict or the escalation of the conflict. It subjugates Gain for Relationship. It is viewed as a weak and unsustainable strategy.

Neville Chamberlin demonstrated the most notorious example of the use of appeasement. Chamberlin was a British Conservative politician who was Prime Minister of the United Kingdom from 1937 to 1940. Chamberlain is best known for his appeasement policy. He signed the Munich Agreement in 1938, conceding the German-speaking Sudetenland region of Czechoslovakia to Germany. The intent of these concessions was to avoid conflict with Adolph Hitler and Germany. When Hitler invaded Poland, the UK declared war on Germany on September 3, 1939, Chamberlain remained Britain's Prime Minister through the first eight months of World War II. After an abysmal performance at the beginning of the war, Chamberlin was replaced as Prime Minister with Winston Churchill.
Accede

To accede is to give one's consent, approval, or adherence by yielding. It requires one to give to a request. Acceding involves becoming a party to an agreement or treaty. The difference between acceding and appeasing is the strategy. The strategy of appeasement is to maintain a harmonious relationship through unilateral concession making. The strategy of acceding is to grant concessions or gain with the purpose a future payback that is not necessarily in kind.

An example of acceding is Berkshire Hathaway CEO Warren Buffett's pledge to give away 99 percent of his wealth to philanthropic causes. Approximately 83 percent of that will go to the Bill & Melinda Gates Foundation and much of the rest will be distributed to the foundations managed by his children. He is a very hands-off philanthropist, preferring to entrust his wealth to those he knows will spend it wisely on worthwhile philanthropic causes.

Buffett has long held the belief that he could do the most good by amassing as much capital as possible during his lifetime and then giving most of it away at the end of his life. He once told the *New York Times*, "I don't believe in dynastic wealth." In 2006, he pledged to give all of his Berkshire Hathaway stock to philanthropic foundations, and in 2010 he and Bill Gates went public with the Giving Pledge, aimed at encouraging billionaires to pledge at least half of their wealth to charity. Buffett is one example but there are many others. A list of extremely wealthy people who have given a majority of their personal wealth to philanthropy can be found at http://givingpledge.org.

Influence

For the purpose of this book we will use the working definition from Robert Cialdini "Weapons of Influence." They promote an individual's propensity to be influenced by a persuader:

- Reciprocity: People tend to return a favor.
- Commitment and Consistency: People do not like to be self-contradictory. Once they commit to an idea or

behavior, they are averse to changing their minds without good reason.

- Social Proof: People will be more open to things they see others doing. For example, seeing others compost their organic waste after finishing a meal may influence them to do so as well.
- Authority: People will tend to obey authority figures.
- Liking: Likeable people are able to sway people with more ease.
- Scarcity: A perceived limitation of availability will generate demand.

Our government's industry of influence with dominant players provides abundant examples of how the use of influence plays out not only in politics but business negotiations as well. Just about any "special" interest group you can think of has a presence in Washington and spends money to maintain that presence. These interest groups spend obscene amounts of money lobbying, which is the other side of the influence coin. Professional advocates lobby members of Congress and government officials on issues on behalf of their clients. The money that industries, companies, unions and other groups spend on lobbying is small compared to what they can reap in return if their lobbyists are successful. The mantra of the lobbyist is "It's not what you know, it's who you know." Success as a lobbyist comes with a combination of knowledge and personal connections.

In a campaign finance system where all the money originates from individuals, political action committees (PACs) control the most "corporate" of money. Controlled by companies, trade associations, unions, issue groups and even politicians these committees' pool contributions from individuals and distribute them to candidates, political parties and other PACs. PACs can also spend money independently on political activities, including advertising and other efforts to support or oppose candidates in an election.

Influence in Washington has many components; Political donations, outside spending and lobbying expenditures of labor unions, corporations and trade groups, as well as the number of lawmakers who have personally invested in them.

Persuade
Persuasion attempts to influence a person's beliefs, attitudes, intentions, motivations, or behaviors. Persuasion is aimed at changing a person's attitude or behavior toward some event, idea, object, or another person, by using the principles of sound argumentation to convey information, feelings, or reasoning. Persuasion is also an often-used tool in the pursuit of personal gains, such as election campaigning, giving a sales pitch, or in trial advocacy. Persuasion can also be interpreted as using one's personal or positional resources to change people's behaviors or attitudes. Systematic persuasion is the process through which attitudes or beliefs are leveraged by appeals to logic and reason. Heuristic persuasion, on the other hand, appeals to habit or emotion.

Collaborate
Collaboration is the process of two or more people or organizations working together to achieve a satisfactory resolution to a problem. Collaboration is very similar to cooperation in that both are opposite of competition. Most collaboration requires leadership, trust, and vision. Collaborative teams can obtain greater resources, recognition, and reward when facing competition for finite resources.

Structured methods of collaboration usually are defined processes, encourage introspection of behavior and communication. These methods specifically aim to increase success through collaborative problem resolving.

Compromise
The Oxford English Dictionary (OED) explains that to compromise is "to arbitrate and settle differences." Implicit in this definition is the process of give and take that usually results in one or both parties not achieving all that is needed or wanted. At best, compromise is suboptimal. Here is a rule of thumb that describes the relationship between compromise and negotiation, "you can have negotiation without compromise,

but you cannot have compromise without negotiation." If two parties practice 'positional negotiating,' or make demands that are markedly different, there is no way to reach an agreement without compromise. Positional negotiation starts with solutions instead of problems. If you can identify the problems in the form of needs, then you can most likely get to an agreement without compromise. The degree of reciprocity governs the worth of the compromise the parties exhibit without sacrificing their real needs. Compromise requires an understanding of the differences between need and want.

Bargain
Bargaining or haggling is a type of negotiation in which the buyer and seller of a good or service debate the price and the terms of the transaction. If the bargaining produces agreement on terms and price, the transaction takes place. Bargaining is an alternative to a fixed price system. Assuming that there is no cost to bargain, the buyer can assess the seller's willingness to sell and the seller the buyer's willingness to spend. It allows for capturing of more value as it allows price discrimination. A seller can charge a higher price to one buyer who is more eager, or a lower price to one that is less eager. Haggling for necessities of daily living has largely disappeared in parts of the world where the cost to haggle exceeds the gain. For expensive items sold to uninformed buyers such as automobiles, bargaining is commonplace. Dickering refers to the same process, albeit with a slightly negative, petty connotation.

Power Play
Power plays provide the ability to influence or outright control the behavior of people. The term "authority" is often used for power perceived as legitimate. Exploitation of power may be seen as evil or unjust, but the exercise of power is accepted as pervasive. Power Plays are the application of negative influences to garner gain. It includes the ability to manipulate, intimidate, deceive and subjugate. Coercive power tends to be the most obvious but least effective form of power because it destroys relationships. It builds resentment and resistance from the people who experience it. Pressure, authority and extreme reliance on leverage are standard tools of coercion.

Excessive use of time, pressure, deception and authority tactics are examples of using coercive power. Extensive use of coercive power is rarely appropriate in a business or political setting. Relying on these forms of power alone will result in a frigid, impoverished style of doing business.

Coerce

To coerce is to attempt to compel by force, intimidation, or authority, especially without regard for individual desire or volition. It intends to bring about concessions through the use of force or other forms of compulsion. Coercion in the negotiating realm doesn't usually involve a physical threat of bodily harm. It is intended to dominate or control, especially by exploiting fear, or anxiety. They may include threats of reprisal and retaliation. Coercion may be applied to career mobility or adverse financial consequences. Coercion is the most extreme tactic employed to extract Gain.

Default Behaviors

Relationship and Gain are rarely mutually exclusive or binary. Occasionally, there are people who do, in fact, demonstrate the extreme at the exclusion of the other. Most of us tend to find ourselves somewhere along the continuum. At one end there is Relationship. It is defined in this context as the connection, bond or feeling for another. The extreme of the Relationship default puts others well being exclusively over self. At the other end of the continuum is Gain, the opposite of Relationship. Whether conscious or unconscious the only tradeoffs in negotiations are at the extremes of Relationship and Gain, or somewhere on the continuum. This dynamic tension between these two components is always in play in negotiations. My purpose in discussing it is to ensure your trade-offs are being made consciously, not unwittingly. Regrettably, most of us have an unconscious default setting of either Gain or Relationship. The problem is not that you have a default, but that this default is mostly unconscious.

In the extreme, the consequences of defaulting to Gain, like a person with too much ego strength and little to no empathy, is that you may be viewed as an intimidator, a taker, a bully or a steamroller. Conversely, if Relationship is the default setting, then you might be seen by your organization as weak, ineffective, a giver or working for other's team.

No drive and no palpable empathy usually leave them unemployed, and in the negotiating arena, it would render them easy prey. Most of us are somewhere in the middle, but you tend to lean one-way or another; leaning toward Gain or Relationship, defaulting to getting more or to maintaining harmony. Defaulting to Relationship or Gain is neither bad nor good. It is what it is.

Whatever your default, recognize that there are consequences. Trade Relationship and Gain consciously, not unwittingly. The issue as it relates to negotiation is one of balance or equilibrium between Relationship and Gain. You'll discuss individual default settings in the Accommodation section, which follows later. For now, understand that you all have varying degrees of propensity to default to either Relationship or Gain. Regrettably, you make mostly unconscious tradeoffs between them.

Adaptability

Adaptability is a measure that will be discussed later. It is the critical Global Five measure of preference for Accommodation or Egocentricity in negotiations. For now simply understand that they exist. Accommodate means focus on living for others. Accommodating people tend to default to relationship. Egocentric means the focus is on living for self. Their default is toward Gain.

Empathy

Empathy is the capacity to understand or feel what another person is experiencing from within another being's frame of reference; that is the capacity to place oneself in another's position. There are many definitions for empathy, which encompass a broad range of emotional states. Types of empathy include emotional empathy and somatic empathy. In the development of human empathy, individual differences appear, ranging from no apparent empathic ability, or empathy, which is harmful to self or others, to well-balanced empathy.

Empathy is the ability of people to recognize and respond to the emotions of others. It's the foundation of both sympathy and compassion. Without empathy, sympathy and compassion are more likely to be inaccurate and may lead to increased friction and resentment. The people who are the targets of sympathy or compassion have heightened sensitivity to actions that are not based on authentic understanding. They may feel that actions such as an act of charity or a kind word are degrading forms of pity. Because they believe that they are not based on an attempt at understanding the recipient's reality. Compassion, real compassion is empathy put into action.

Psychopathy, also known as sociopathy is traditionally defined as a personality disorder characterized by persistent antisocial behavior, impaired <u>empathy</u>, and remorse, and <u>bold</u>, disinhibited egotistical <u>traits</u>. A large body of research suggests that psychopathy is associated with atypical responses to expressions of fear and sadness. A psychopath's responsiveness to expressions of fear and impairments of empathy are pronounced.

The model, formulated by Christopher J. Patrick suggests that psychopathy emphasizes three observable characteristics to varying degrees:

- Boldness. Low fear including stress-tolerance, toleration of unfamiliarity and danger, and high self-confidence and social assertiveness.
- Disinhibition. Poor impulse control including problems with planning and foresight, lacking urge control, demand for immediate gratification, and poor behavioral restraints.
- Meanness. Lacking empathy and close attachments with others, disdain of close attachments, use of cruelty to gain empowerment, exploitative tendencies, defiance of authority, and destructive excitement seeking

If you find yourself engaged with someone who exhibits these characteristics, exit the relationship if at all possible. Remember that negotiating is a problem resolution process that can, that can temporarily settle issues between people and groups of people. And a successful negotiation results in all parties securing what they truly need without irreparable damage to the relationship. A Social Darwinist does not play by these definitions, so why would you attempt to deal with one. If you find yourself involved with a person exhibiting these traits terminate any dealing with them. If you cannot, then recognize that you are in a vulnerable position and proceed with extreme caution.

Propensity to Find Opportunities to Negotiate

Why do some people seek out opportunities to negotiate, but others avoid negotiating as if it were the plague? This penchant tends to track along the lines of a person's default setting for Relationship over Gain. The reciprocal is true as well. Is this a merely a blinding flash of the obvious? No, it's buried in the psyche of each. Most people who avoid the negotiations tend to be givers and have distaste for this arena.

Perspective on Availability of Resources

There is a paradox embedded in society that impacts nearly every aspect of the socioeconomic system. It revolves around the diametrically opposite worldviews. One side evolved out of humanity's past, while the other is a relatively recent arrival. Most people unwittingly have one of these defaults that drive their attitudes and approach to negotiations. To understand how the perspectives of scarcity and plenty work, you need to understand what they are and how they evolved.

At the core of the conflict are the efforts to preserve a traditional mentality of scarcity in today's world, which is built to a large extent from a mindset of plenty.

The mentality of scarcity has been dominant through most of human history and is probably still the perspective held by the majority of people today. The Scarcity mentality sees the wealth of the world as finite and limited--there is only one fixed pie and the larger the slice appropriated by one individual or group, the smaller the resulting slices left over for others. Those who can acquire the greatest slice of the pie also gain the greatest power and are best able to gain additional wealth and power. In a primarily agrarian society, where the use of land is the primary means of producing wealth, wealth is best expressed as the possession of land. Equating wealth with control over the means of production expands the usefulness of property as a means of acquiring power far beyond the pure financial value of wealth.

The industrial age created whole new sources and definitions of wealth independent of land ownership, creating in the process the potential to endlessly expand the amount of wealth available to society. New manufacturers are designed to fill any shortfall in supply. Supply will rise to meet any demand--if people want something enough to pay for it, someone will find a way. More important to the mentality of plenty is expanding the variety of products and wealth.

Some of the most profitable businesses in the current economy, like Apple Computer, Microsoft and Facebook were launched out of garages or dorm rooms with almost no start-up capital. Currently, the preferred path to wealth is not to compete, to take a slice of the real pie away from someone else, but rather to create a whole new pie from which it is much easier to acquire a generous slice. Given the emergence of geopolitical factors such as the resent rise of nationalism, global climate change, exhaustion of nonrenewable resources and global population explosion, we may see a shift toward a perspective of scarcity.

My point in raising this issue is not that either is right or wrong, perfect or flawed, they just are. In negotiations, if you approach situations from a perspective of scarcity, then in your mind the pie at stake is fixed, and the problem becomes how to ensure you optimize your portion. This is the realm of positional negotiation. On the other hand, if you have a penchant for approaching negotiations from the perspective of abundance, then you will tend to work to collaborate to expand the dimensions of the pie. Both approaches have pluses and minuses as a sole guiding principle. Recognition of your default setting is a great first step in expanding your perspective. The approach should be driven by the situation and context, not your worldview. Sometimes the negotiating pie is fixed and sometimes it's not.

FALLACIES OF LOGIC:

These represent arguments that are intend to be a substitute for logic, but are flawed. Let's look at each and connect the to negotiating situations starting with the ***hasty generalization.*** It draws conclusions from inadequate evidence. Suppose someone makes a claim like, "My product provides both superior performance." Then the person gives only two planned examples to support the opinion. That's not enough, because others might not feel the same way for a multitude of reasons. A person who makes such a statement is indulging in a hasty generalization. **Stereotyping** is another form of hasty generalization. It happens, for example, when someone says, "All Asian's are tough negotiators." Such a sweeping claim about all members of a particular ethnic, religious, racial, or political group is stereotyping. Yet another kind of stereotyping is sexism, which occurs when someone discriminates against another person based on gender. For example, when an observer a negotiation involving a women and a man, if a person makes a comment about "men are much better negotiators than women," the person is guilty of a combination of stereotyping and sexism—both components of hasty generalization.

A *false analogy* draws a comparison in which the differences outweigh the similarities or the similarities are irrelevant. For example, "You're investment in this venture is as secure as the Rock of Gibraltar" is a false analogy. An investment isn't an iconic limestone peak. Also, comparing the security an investment to the permanence of a peak are not the same. Homespun analogies like this have an air of wisdom about them but tend to fall apart when examined closely.

Begging the question tries to offer proof by simply using another version of the argument itself. This is also called circular reasoning. For example, "Our firm should be your trusted advisor because we are the oldest accountancy firm in the world" begs the question. Trusted advisor is synonymous with oldest, since our firm is the oldest it's the most trusted, so the statement goes around in a circle, getting nowhere. Evidence of the claimed trusted advisor is missing. Here's another example with a different twist. "We been trusted advisor over the years because we have been in business longer than anyone else." Here, the support for the second part of the statement is the argument in the first part of the statement. Obviously, since trusted advisor is essential, and can be earned through performance not longevity. And here's yet another example: "All foreign supplies do business only on price." This time, the problem is the unstated assumption that foreign suppliers supposed lower price, not the price that attracts customers. Yet the audience can't be assumed to share the opinion that foreign suppliers are all price cutters based upon the arguments presented.

An *irrelevant argument* reaches a conclusion that doesn't follow from the premises. It's also called a non sequitur (Latin for "it does not follow"). This happens when a conclusion doesn't follow from the premises. Here's an example: "XYZ Company has been in business for years, so they'll make a great business partner." What does being in business for years have to do with being a great business partner? Are there other equally important criteria that will indicate that XYZ should be selected as a business partner? Absent from the logic are requirements of a partner like; innovation, reliability, fiscally sound, price competitiveness, product quality, service level … .

A *false cause* assumes that because two events are related in time, the first caused the second. It's also known as post hoc, ergo propter hoc (Latin for "after this, therefore because of this") or the Butterfly effect. For example, if someone claims that a since we switched to the new logo productivity has fallen, that person is connecting two events that have no causal relationship to each other. One must be careful that the two are connected. Cause and Effect can lead to the ripple effect though. When many events are related and can be traced back to each other much like the "to build a mousetrap game." This is a major cause of jumping to a conclusion for many that do not carefully look at the outcome and logically reason out the problem.

A **red herring** tries to distract attention from one issue by introducing a second that is unrelated to the first. It's sometimes call ignoring the question. By using an irrelevant issue, a person hopes to distract that audience, just as putting a herring in the path of a bloodhound would distract if from the scent it has been told to follow. This is very big in the political arena.

An **argument to the person** means attacking the person making the argument rather than the argument itself. It's also known as the **ad hominem** (Latin for "to the man") attack. When a person's appearance, habits, or character is criticized instead of the merits of that person's argument, the attack is a fallacy. Here's an example: "We'd take her seriously if she didn't have such an aversion to the truth." Most people when losing a debate do this "You always think you are right, but you are not!" This fallacy of logic is widely used in the political arena.

Guilt by association means that a person's arguments, ideas, or opinions lack merit because of that person's activities, interests, or companions. For example, here's the fallacy in operation: "Hillary is married to Bill, who had scandals in the past. This makes her unfit to be president." The fact that Bill was involved in scandals and Hillary is married to Bill has nothing to do with his ability to be the president.

Jumping on the bandwagon means something is right or permissible because "everyone does it." It's also called ***ad populum*** (Latin for "to the people"). This fallacy operates in statements such as "All of your competitors are using XYZ Software." Just because one can do something doesn't make it right to do. Also done as justification of actions.

The following fallacies are similar in that they present a limited selective view of reality and the truth. Using ***false or irrelevant authority*** means citing the opinion of someone who has no expertise in the subject at hand. This fallacy attempts to transfer prestige from one area to another. Many television commercials rely on this tactic—a famous tennis player praising a brand of motor oil or a popular movie start lauding a brand of cheese. ***Card-stacking*** ignores evidence of the other side of the questions. It's also known as special pleading. From all the available facts, only those that will build the best (or worst) possible case are used. Customer testimonials, promotional literature and fall into this fallacy. ***Taking something out of context*** deliberately distorts an idea or a fact by removing it from its previously surrounding details.

The ***either-or*** fallacy offers only two alternatives when more exist. This fallacy is also called false dilemma. Such fallacies tend to touch on emotional issues and can therefore seem accurate until analyzed. For example in negotiations this fallacy of logic is manifested in the take-it-or-leave tactic, "Either take my offer or I'm walking away." If tested the tactic may just be a rouse and more bargaining is possible. However, I may be a last and final offer.

Appeal to ignorance ties to make an incorrect argument based on its never having been shown to be false—or, the reverse, an incorrect argument based on its not yet having been proven true. Such appeals can be very persuasive because they prey on people's superstitions or lack of knowledge. Such appeals are often stated in the fuzzy language of double negatives. Here's an example: "Because it hasn't been proven that eating food X does not cause cancer, we can assume that is does." In truth, the absence of opposing evidence proves nothing. Telling half the story or giving half the information, then drawing a conclusion from that.

Ambiguity and equivocation are statements that can be interpreted in more than one way, thus concealing the truth. For example, suppose a person is asked, "Is she doing a good job?" and the person answers with "She's performing as expected." Such an answer is open to positive or negative interpretation. A similar example of this fallacy is when the question "Have you made any progress?" is answered by "We've held some meetings." Most who do this answer with nonspecific answers, never directly answering the question. Avoidance is the key to identifying this.

So, what can you do to mitigate the negative effects of your negotiating style? If you're generally unhappy with your negotiated results, it's time to take control and Stop Blaming the Fish.

PERSONALITY TRAIT MAPS

The following Maps examine all of the personality traits defined in the Global Five along in the area identified as **TYPE**.

DEFAULT measures your propensity to default to Gain or Relationship. Your accommodation score drives it. The reason you use this standard is that the Gain/Relationship tension has the greatest impact on the negotiating process. As you examine your Global Five results notice the

PRIMARY TYPE. That measure identifies the element that you scored most strongly.

STRENGTHS and **LIABILITIES** refer to those negotiating behaviors that can be your assets and liabilities.

CUES are behaviors that indicate your personality traits to others in a negotiation.

TYPE: SLOEI   **DEFAULT: GAIN**

Assets	Liabilities	Cues
– Generates lots of logical solutions – Out-of-the box thinker – Makes opinion known – Decisive	– Can miss critical details – Ideas may be too complex – May have trouble with authority – May be overwhelming – Not inclusionary – May make heat-of-the-moment decisions – Can mislead self – May be inflexible – Can be impulsive. May react before thinking things through – May get emotional	– Talks to think – Deals mainly with concepts, avoids details – Values objectivity over subjectivity – Quick to make up their mind – Responds Emotionally or unconsciously

TYPE: SLOAI   **DEFAULT: RELATIONSHIP**

Assets	Liabilities	Cues
– Resolves conflicts – Usually good communicator – Motivational – Makes opinion known – Decisive – Has a people perspective	– Tends to decide based on own biases – Has a hard time staying neutral, can get sucked into the problem – May be overwhelming – May not be inclusionary – May make heat-of-the-moment decisions – Can mislead self – Can be impulsive. May react before thinking things through – May get emotional	– Talks to think – Deals mainly with concepts, avoids details – Considers people issues above the bottom line – Quick to make up their mind – Responds Emotionally or unconsciously

TYPE: SLOEN   **DEFAULT: GAIN**

Assets	Liabilities	Cues
– Traditional thinker – Plays by the principles – Dependable – Makes opinion known – Decisive – Concrete	– Predictable – May not be an innovator – Usually short term thinker – May be overwhelming – Not inclusionary – Finds it difficult to conceptualize – May be inflexible – Can be impulsive. May react before thinking things through – May get emotional	– Talks to think – Deals mainly with facts, concepts are a waste of time – Values objectivity over subjectivity – Quick to make up their mind – Responds Emotionally or unconsciously

TYPE: SLOAN   **DEFAULT: RELATIONSHIP**

Assets	Liabilities	Cues
– Traditional thinker – Plays by the principles – Dependable – Makes opinion known – Decisive – Has a people perspective	– Predictable – May not be an innovator – Usually short term thinker – May be overwhelming – Not inclusionary – Acutely sensitive to peoples feelings – Can be impulsive. May react before thinking things through – May get emotional	– Talks to think – Deals mainly with facts, concepts are a waste of time – Considers people issues above the bottom line – Quick to make up their mind – Responds Emotionally or unconsciously

TYPE: SLUEI   **DEFAULT: GAIN**

Assets	Liabilities	Cues
– Generates lots of logical solutions – Out-of-the box thinker – Quick on their feet	– Can miss critical details – Ideas may be too complex – May have trouble with authority – Likely to talk too much – May talk in circles – Finds it difficult to accept differing perspectives – Can be a perfectionist – Can be impulsive – May react before thinking things through - May get emotional	– Talks to think – Deals mainly with concepts, avoids details – Values objectivity over subjectivity – Slow to decide in order to make the best decision – Responds Emotionally or unconsciously

TYPE: SLUAI   **DEFAULT: RELATIONSHIP**

Assets	Liabilities	Cues
– Resolves conflicts – Usually good communicator – Motivational – Quick on their feet – Defends underdogs	– Tends to decide based on own biases – Has a hard time staying neutral, can get sucked into the problem – Likely to talk too much – May talk in circles – Finds it difficult to accept differing perspective – Can be impulsive. May react before thinking things through – May get emotional	– Talks to think – Deals mainly with concepts, avoids details – Considers people issues above the bottom line – Slow to decide in order to make the best decision – Responds Emotionally or unconsciously

TYPE: SLUEN   DEFAULT: GAIN

Assets	Liabilities	Cues
– Can deal with ambiguity – Good in crisis – Resourceful – Quick on their feet – Concrete	– Unpredictable – May lose energy when crisis passes – May not consider the consequences of their – Likely to talk too much – May talk in circles – Finds it difficult to conceptualize – Can be a perfectionist – Can be impulsive. May react before thinking things through – May get emotional	– Talks to think – Deals mainly with facts, concepts are a waste of time – Values objectivity over subjectivity – Slow to decide in order to make the best decision – Responds Emotionally or unconsciously

TYPE: SLUAN   DEFAULT: RELATIONSHIP

Assets	Liabilities	Cues
– Can deal with ambiguity – Good in crisis – Resourceful – Quick on their feet – Defends underdogs	– Unpredictable – May lose energy when crisis passes – May not consider the consequences of their behavior – Likely to talk too much – May talk in circles – Acutely sensitive to people's feelings – Can be impulsive. May react before thinking things through – May get emotional	– Talks to think – Deals mainly with facts, concepts are a waste of time – Considers people issues above the bottom line – Slow to decide in order to make the best decision – Responds Emotionally or unconsciously

TYPE: RLOEI — DEFAULT: GAIN

Assets	Liabilities	Cues
– Generates lots of logical solutions – Out-of-the box thinker – Gets more information than they give – May be perceived as a good listener	– Can miss critical details – Ideas may be too complex – May have trouble with authority – May not appear to be engaged fully – May make heat-of-the-moment decisions – Can mislead self – May be inflexible – Can be impulsive. May react before thinking things through – May get emotional	– Thinks before talking – Deals mainly with concepts, avoids details – Values objectivity over subjectivity – Quick to make up their mind – Responds Emotionally or unconsciously

TYPE: RLOAI — DEFAULT: RELATIONSHIP

Assets	Liabilities	Cues
– Resolves conflicts – Usually good communicator – Motivational – Gets more information than they give – May be perceived as a good listener – Has a people perspective	– Tends to decide based on own biases – Has a hard time staying neutral, can get sucked into the problem – May not appear to be engaged fully – May make heat-of-the-moment decisions – Can mislead self – Can be impulsive. May react before thinking things through – May get emotional	– Thinks before talking – Deals mainly with concepts, avoids details – Considers people issues above the bottom line – Quick to make up their mind – Responds Emotionally or unconsciously

95

TYPE: RLOEN   DEFAULT: GAIN

Assets	Liabilities	Cues
– Traditional thinker – Plays by the principles – Dependable – Gets more information – May be a good listener – Concrete	– Predictable – May not be an innovator – Usually short term thinker – May not appear to be engaged fully – Finds it difficult to conceptualize – May be inflexible – Can be impulsive. May react before thinking things through – May get emotional	– Thinks before talking – Deals mainly with facts, concepts are a waste of time – Values objectivity over subjectivity – Quick to make up their mind – Responds Emotionally or unconsciously

TYPE: RLOAN   DEFAULT: RELATIONSHIP

Assets	Liabilities	Cues
– Traditional thinker – Plays by the principles – Dependable – Gets more information than they give – May be perceived as a good listener – Has a people perspective	– Predictable – May not be an innovator – Usually short term thinker – May not appear to be engaged fully – Acutely sensitive to peoples feelings – Can be impulsive. May react before thinking things through – May get emotional	– Thinks before talking – Deals mainly with facts, concepts are a waste of time – Considers people issues above the bottom line – Quick to make up their mind – Responds Emotionally or unconsciously

TYPE: RLUEI — DEFAULT: GAIN

Assets	Liabilities	Cues
– Generates lots of logical solutions – Out-of-the box thinker – Doesn't shoot from the hip – Can be a perfectionist	– Can miss critical details – Ideas may be too complex – May have trouble with authority – May come across as aloof – Finds it difficult to accept differing perspectives – Can be impulsive. May react before thinking things through – May get emotional	– Thinks before talking – Deals mainly with concepts, avoids details – Values objectivity over subjectivity – Slow to decide in order to make the best decision – Responds Emotionally or unconsciously

TYPE: RLUAI — DEFAULT: RELATIONSHIP

Assets	Liabilities	Cues
– Resolves conflicts – Usually good communicator – Motivational – Doesn't shoot from the hip – Defends underdogs	– Tends to decide based on own biases – Has a hard time staying neutral can get sucked into the problem – May come across as aloof or detached – Finds it difficult to accept differing perspectives – Can be impulsive. May react before thinking things through – May get emotional	– Thinks before talking – Deals mainly with concepts, avoids details – Considers people issues above the bottom line – Slow to decide in order to make the best decision – Responds Emotionally or unconsciously

TYPE: RLUEN   DEFAULT: GAIN

Assets	Liabilities	Cues
– Can deal with ambiguity – Good in crisis – Resourceful – Doesn't shoot from the hip – Concrete	– Unpredictable – May lose energy when crisis passes – May not consider the consequences of their behavior – May come across as aloof or detached – Finds it difficult to conceptualize – Can be a perfectionist – Can be impulsive. May react before thinking things through – May get emotional	– Thinks before talking – Deals mainly with facts, concepts are a waste of time – Values objectivity over subjectivity – Slow to decide in order to make the best decision – Responds Emotionally or unconsciously

TYPE: RLUAN   DEFAULT: RELATIONSHIP

Assets	Liabilities	Cues
– Can deal with ambiguity – Good in crisis – Resourceful – Doesn't shoot from the hip – Defends underdogs	– Unpredictable – May lose energy when crisis passes – May not consider the consequences of their behavior – May come across as aloof or detached – Acutely sensitive to peoples feelings – Can be impulsive. May react before thinking things through – Can be emotional	– Thinks before talking – Deals mainly with facts, concepts are a waste of time – Considers people issues above the bottom line – Slow to decide in order to make the best decision – Responds Emotionally or unconsciously

TYPE: SCOEI — DEFAULT: GAIN

Assets	Liabilities	Cues
– Generates lots of logical solutions – Out-of-the box thinker – Makes opinion known – Decisive	– Can miss critical details – Ideas may be too complex – May have trouble with authority – May be overwhelming – Not inclusionary – May make heat-of-the-moment decisions – Can mislead self – May be inflexible – Can appear to be overly pensive	– Talks to think – Deals mainly with concepts, avoids details – Values objectivity over subjectivity – Quick to make up their mind – Responds in a calm, unemotional and measured fashion

TYPE: SCOAI — DEFAULT: RELATIONSHIP

Assets	Liabilities	Cues
– Resolves conflicts – Usually good communicator – Motivational – Makes opinion known – Decisive – Has a people perspective	– Tends to decide based on own biases – Has a hard time staying neutral, can get sucked into the problem – May be overwhelming – May not be inclusionary – May make heat-of-the-moment decisions – Can mislead self – Can appear to be overly pensive	– Talks to think – Deals mainly with concepts, avoids details – Considers people issues above the bottom line – Quick to make up their mind – Responds in a calm, unemotional and measured fashion

TYPE: SCOEN   **DEFAULT: GAIN**

Assets	Liabilities	Cues
– Traditional thinker – Plays by the principles – Dependable – Makes opinion known – Decisive – Concrete	– Predictable – May not be an innovator – Usually short term thinker – May be overwhelming – Not inclusionary – Finds it difficult to conceptualize – May be inflexible – Can appear to be overly pensive	– Talks to think – Deals mainly with facts, concepts are a waste of time – Values objectivity over subjectivity – Quick to make up their mind – Responds in a calm, unemotional and measured fashion

TYPE: SCOAN   **DEFAULT: RELATIONSHIP**

Assets	Liabilities	Cues
– Traditional thinker – Plays by the principles – Dependable – Makes opinion known – Decisive – Has a people perspective	– Predictable – May not be an innovator – Usually short term thinker – May be overwhelming – Not inclusionary – Acutely sensitive to peoples feelings – Can appear to be overly pensive	– Talks to think – Deals mainly with facts, concepts are a waste of time – Considers people issues above the bottom line – Quick to make up their mind – Responds in a calm, unemotional and measured fashion

TYPE: SCUEI   **DEFAULT: GAIN**

Assets	Liabilities	Cues
– Generates lots of logical solutions – Out-of-the box thinker – Quick on their feet	– Can miss critical details – Ideas may be too complex – May have trouble with authority – Likely to talk too much – May talk in circles – Finds it difficult to accept differing perspectives – Can be a perfectionist – Can appear to be overly pensive	– Talks to think – Deals mainly with concepts, avoids details – Values objectivity ov subjectivity – Slow to decide in order to make the best decision – Responds in a calm, unemotional and measured fashion

TYPE: SCUAI   **DEFAULT: RELATIONSHIP**

Assets	Liabilities	Cues
– Resolves conflicts – Usually good communicator – Motivational – Quick on their feet – Defends underdogs	– Tends to decide based on own biases – Has a hard time staying neutral, can get sucked into the problem – Likely to talk too much – May talk in circles – Finds it difficult to accept differing perspective – Can appear to be overly pensive	– Talks to think – Deals mainly with concepts, avoids details – Considers people issues above the bottom line – Slow to decide in order to make the best decision – Responds in a calm, unemotional and measured fashion

TYPE: SCUEN   **DEFAULT: GAIN**

Assets	Liabilities	Cues
– Can deal with ambiguity – Good in crisis – Resourceful – Quick on their feet – Concrete	– Unpredictable – May lose energy when crisis passes – May not consider the consequences of their – Likely to talk too much – May talk in circles – Finds it difficult to conceptualize – Can be a perfectionist – Can appear to be overly pensive	– Talks to think – Deals mainly with facts, concepts are a waste of time – Values objectivity over subjectivity – Slow to decide in order to make the best decision – Responds in a calm, unemotional and measured fashion

TYPE: SCUAN   **DEFAULT: RELATIONSHIP**

Assets	Liabilities	Cues
– Can deal with ambiguity – Good in crisis – Resourceful – Quick on their feet – Defends underdogs	– Unpredictable – May lose energy when crisis passes – May not consider the consequences of their behavior – Likely to talk too much – May talk in circles – Acutely sensitive to peoples feelings – Can appear to be overly pensive	– Talks to think – Deals mainly with facts, concepts are a waste of time – Considers people issues above the bottom line – Slow to decide in order to make the best decision – Responds in a calm, unemotional and measured fashion

TYPE: RCOEI   DEFAULT: GAIN

Assets	Liabilities	Cues
– Generates lots of logical solutions – Out-of-the box thinker – Gets more information than they give – May be perceived as a good listener	– Can miss critical details – Ideas may be too complex – May have trouble with authority – May not appear to be engaged fully – May make heat-of-the-moment decisions – Can mislead self – May be inflexible – Can appear to be overly pensive	– Thinks before talking – Deals mainly with concepts, avoids details – Values objectivity over subjectivity – Quick to make up their mind – Responds in a calm, unemotional and measured fashion

TYPE: RCOAI   DEFAULT: RELATIONSHIP

Assets	Liabilities	Cues
– Resolves conflicts – Usually good communicator – Motivational – Gets more information than they give – May be perceived as a good listener – Has a people perspective	– Tends to decide based on own biases – Has a hard time staying neutral, can get sucked into the problem – May not appear to be engaged fully – May make heat-of-the-moment decisions – Can mislead self – Can appear to be overly pensive	– Thinks before talking – Deals mainly with concepts, avoids details – Considers people issues above the bottom line – Quick to make up their mind – Responds in a calm, unemotional and measured fashion

TYPE: RCOEN   **DEFAULT: GAIN**

Assets	Liabilities	Cues
– Traditional thinker – Plays by the principles – Dependable – Gets more information – May be a good listener – Concrete	– Predictable – May not be an innovator – Usually short term thinker – May not appear to be engaged fully – Finds it difficult to conceptualize – May be inflexible – Can appear to be overly pensive	– Thinks before talking – Deals mainly with facts, concepts are a waste of time – Values objectivity over subjectivity – Quick to make up their mind – Responds in a calm, unemotional and measured fashion

TYPE: RCOAN   **DEFAULT: RELATIONSHIP**

Assets	Liabilities	Cues
– Traditional thinker – Plays by the principles – Dependable – Gets more information than they give – May be perceived as a good listener – Has a people perspective	– Predictable – May not be an innovator – Usually short term thinker – May not appear to be engaged fully – Acutely sensitive to peoples feelings – Can appear to be overly pensive	– Thinks before talking – Deals mainly with facts, concepts are a waste of time – Considers people issues above the bottom line – Quick to make up their mind – Responds in a calm, unemotional and measured fashion

TYPE: RCUEI — DEFAULT: GAIN

Assets	Liabilities	Cues
– Generates lots of logical solutions – Out-of-the box thinker – Doesn't shoot from the hip – Can be a perfectionist	– Can miss critical details – Ideas may be too complex – May have trouble with authority – May come across as aloof – Finds it difficult to accept differing perspectives – Can appear to be overly pensive	Thinks before talking – Deals mainly with concepts, avoids details – Values objectivity over subjectivity – Slow to decide in order to make the best decision – Responds in a calm, unemotional and measured fashion

TYPE: RCUAI — DEFAULT: RELATIONSHIP

Assets	Liabilities	Cues
– Resolves conflicts – Usually good communicator – Motivational – Doesn't shoot from the hip – Defends underdogs	– Tends to decide based on own biases – Has a hard time staying neutral can get sucked into the problem – May come across as aloof or detached – Finds it difficult to accept differing perspectives – Can appear to be overly pensive	– Thinks before talking – Deals mainly with concepts, avoids details – Considers people issues above the bottom line – Slow to decide in order to make the best decision – Responds in a calm, unemotional and measured fashion

TYPE: RCUEN   **DEFAULT: GAIN**

Assets	Liabilities	Cues
– Can deal with ambiguity – Good in crisis – Resourceful – Doesn't shoot from the hip – Concrete	– Unpredictable – May lose energy when crisis passes – May not consider the consequences of their behavior – May come across as aloof or detached – Finds it difficult to conceptualize – Can be a perfectionist – Can appear to be overly pensive	– Thinks before talking – Deals mainly with facts, concepts are a waste of time – Values objectivity over subjectivity – Slow to decide in order to make the best decision – Responds in a calm, unemotional and measured fashion

TYPE: RCUAN   **DEFAULT: RELATIONSHIP**

Assets	Liabilities	Cues
– Can deal with ambiguity – Good in crisis – Resourceful – Doesn't shoot from the hip – Defends underdogs	– Unpredictable – May lose energy when crisis passes – May not consider the consequences of their behavior – May come across as aloof or detached – Acutely sensitive to peoples feelings – Can appear to be overly pensive	– Thinks before talking – Deals mainly with facts, concepts are a waste of time – Considers people issues above the bottom line – Slow to decide in order to make the best decision – Responds in a calm, unemotional and measured fashion

CORRELATIONS OF GLOBAL FIVE AND MBTI

For those of you who might be curious, the following table is intended to assist you in correlating your Global Five results to MBTI:

Element	Global Five Notation	MBTI Notation	Correlation
Extroversion	**S**ocial/**R**eserve	Introvert/Extrovert	High
Emotional Stability	**C**alm/**L**imbic	Feeling/Thinking	Very Low
Orderliness	**O**rganized/ Unstructured	Judging/Perceiver	High
Accommodation	**A**ccommodating/ Egocentric	Feeling/Thinking	Medium
Intellect	**N**on-curious/ Inquisitive	Sensing/Intuitive	Medium High

CPSIA information can be obtained
at www.ICGtesting.com
Printed in the USA
BVHW041940020120
568408BV00004B/6/P